SEEDS OF SENSITIVITY

SEEDS OF SENSITIVITY

Deepening Your
Spiritual Life

ROBERT J. WICKS

AVE MARIA PRESS
NOTRE DAME, INDIANA 46556

Contents

For persons without guile
who purify the air for the rest of us.

Introduction

Edwina Gately, who works with homeless and abused women, once told a story that went something like this:

> Once upon a time there was a country ruled by a king. The country was invaded and the king was killed but his children were rescued by servants and hidden away. The smallest, an infant daughter, was reared by a peasant family. They didn't know she was the king's daughter. She had become the peasant's daughter and she dug potatoes and lived in poverty.
>
> One day an old woman came out of the forest and approached the young woman who was digging potatoes. The old woman asked her: "Do you know who you are?" And the young woman said, "Yes, I'm the farmer's daughter and a potato digger." The old woman said: "No, no, you are the daughter of the king." And the potato digger said: "I'm the daughter of the king?" "Yes, that's who you are!" And the old woman disappeared back into the forest.
>
> After the old woman left, the young woman still dug potatoes but she dug them differently. It was the way she held her shoulders and it was the light in her eyes because she knew who she was. She knew she was the daughter of the king.[1]

The central gospel message she conveys in this story is empowerment. She is reminding us that in following Christ: "We must tell people who they are. We must go from place to place saying to the dispossessed and to the lonely and the downtrodden, 'Do you know who you are?'"[2] Instead of retreating in this oftentimes harsh world we must be *sensitive* enough to reach out to the poor, the spiritually hungry, and the emotionally deprived so they may carry themselves with a sense of dignity—even though they may still be digging potatoes. But obviously, this is easier said than done. While the call to be a sensitively compassionate person is clear, so are the perils!

Being sensitive to others in the abstract sounds lovely. However, in reality, it can be quite difficult. The natural temptation today for most of us is to pull back, concentrate on our own needs, and deal with our own worries, insecurities, and daily stresses.

Yet, solely focusing on our own security and sense of well-being won't produce peace for ourselves either. The answer doesn't lie in avoiding involvement with others but in learning *how* to be sensitive to them in a way that will give others—and us—new life.

When we view the lives of people, both in history and from our own families or neighborhoods, who have responded sensitively to the emotional, spiritual, social, and physical needs of others, we see that they often possess inner peace and joy. Unlike those of us who narrow our vision or merely give compulsively to those in need, such persons have found ways to risk sensitivity no matter how harsh the times. In turn their attitude and actions demonstrate that they can see how this attentiveness to others is connected with increased self-awareness and a deep sensitivity to God in prayer.

As a result, if we wish to respond to the gospel call to empower others in a way in which we can experience the peace of God as well today, we need a threefold commitment to sensitivity, a *total* sensitivity to self, others, and God. This must certainly include a willingness to be aware of others in ways that go beyond the usual limits of our so-called openness. But, this in turn, must also be based on a ruthlessly honest appreciation of who we are now and who we might become with a bit more courage, humility, and prayer.

This is sensitivity in its totality. This is, I think, an example of true spirituality. And this is, I believe, what we are called to do and be in today's harsh world. To pierce the darkness by being sensitive persons despite all the forces which are present to prevent such an attitude from flourishing is a call worth hearing and embracing today. If we want peace, and if we want joy, nothing else, nothing less, will do.

Sensitivity to Ourselves

Being a sensitive person isn't just a matter of trying to develop those talents which will help us to better attend to others. A sensitive attitude is a seamless garment which begins with an ability to be more sensitive to *ourselves*. Not realizing this can prevent us from being a fully helpful presence to others. In addition, a lack of self-awareness may be dangerous to our own emotional and spiritual well-being. This is particularly evident when we look at a person whose vocation and whole life involves helping others.

For instance, at this point my clinical practice is limited to professionals in full-time ministry, mental health, and medicine. When I sit with such caring professionals in distress (particularly the ones in ministry), at about the tenth session the same feeling always seems to overwhelm me.

Even though I have heard each of them catalogue their many errors in judgment, past moral lapses, and their major sources of shame and guilt, I still always have the same feeling of sadness at this point in the therapy. It causes me to reflect: "If only you could see yourself now as I see you. If only you could see how wonderful and good you are and were able to appreciate, to some small degree, the gentle and healing presence you have been to so many people in the world." And my hope is that at some point during the therapy they will achieve this recognition.

Obviously this failure to appreciate the goodness of God in themselves while simultaneously seeing it in others is not limited to the talented and caring persons who come in to see me for treatment. I think the same can be said of all of us who wish to be sensitive and live a life that is both centered and meaningful. If we want to pierce the darkness of callousness within and around us in order to embrace the peace that is always present, always possible, we must be willing to appreciate ourselves and our God in new refreshing ways. Otherwise, we are not going to make it as compassionate people. It is as simple as that.

With this in mind, the first section of this book will be on sensitivity to self, focusing on such areas as: unlearning, uncovering and lessening our own defensiveness, sowing the seeds of healthy self-love, letting go, being in the now, the value of experiencing "deep gratitude," and the need for a simple sense of perspective.

Sensitivity to Others

The second section of this book builds on the material on sensitivity to self by presenting a number of essential elements of sensitivity to others. This will enable us to be more aware of others and their needs, as well as on how to further learn about ourselves in the process of reaching out to them. In pursuit of this, a number of practical issues and techniques will be offered.

In the chapter "Seeds of Sensitivity" the topics will include: maintaining a listening stance, how to de-emphasize the need for success in our lives and tolerate failure, the importance of perseverance, uncovering and facing obstacles to sensitivity, and the important role of humor in maintaining perspective. The second chapter in this section, "A Healing Sensitive Stance," will continue to expand on how we can be more open to others and stand with them in difficult times. Topics here will include: the value of encouraging people to "tell their story," helping people to summarize the main issues and difficulties they are facing when they are confused or in conflict, and walking with others in darkness.

Deep Sensitivity—A Renewed Openness to God

Finally, all of this increased self-awareness and new attention to others is connected to and founded on a "deep sensitivity." This can only happen when our awareness of a covenant with God is so real that our words of prayer imperceptibly become acts of gentle, concrete compassion.

In other words, our time in silence and solitude with God must reconnect us with others. Thus our time with them can be seen as a form of "street spirituality," awakening or renewing our sensitivity to both the people we touch and ourselves as well.

In the two chapters in this section the emphasis is on our need to be sensitive to God. The more we are centered the less we are cynical, passive, or involved in an undisciplined activism leading to "burnout." A "street spirituality" which involves both a vibrant prayer life and a prayerful involvement with others is encouraged. To support this theme a candid coverage of the common reasons why people don't pray is presented so these resistances can be faced, understood, and removed—an important undertaking since our relationship with God is at the core of our relationships with self and others.

Following this, we will examine how to confront the psychological and spiritual darkness in our lives. To support this process, attention is given to: ways to clarify our image of God and our relationship with God, considering our faith when reviewing our daily activities, spiritual discernment and psychological clarity, and a renewed appreciation of God's grace.

Piercing the Darkness: Sensitivity in a Harsh World

Rabbi Abraham Joshua Heschel seems to clearly understand why sensitivity is both essential yet avoided when he notes that:

> [A person's] plight is not due to the fear of nonbeing, to the fear of death, but to the fear of living. … The fear of living arises most commonly out of experiences of failure or insult or having gone astray or having been rebuffed. It is rooted in the encounter with other human beings, in not knowing how to be with other human beings, in the inability or refusal to communicate, but above all in the failure to live in

complete involvement with what transcends our living.[3]

To be sensitive in today's secular, security-conscious society is a reflective way of living, both noble and filled with challenge. We can't afford to be naive, hesitant, or compulsive in our awareness and interactions with others and God, otherwise our fears will overtake us. Yet, if we seed our sensitivity with knowledge and humility, we can greet the presence of God in others, ourselves, and in prayer in a way that will make our life more simple, meaningful ... maybe even more holy. And it is with this philosophy that *Seeds of Sensitivity* was written, and it is in this spirit that I share this book with you.

Robert J. Wicks
Loyola College in Maryland

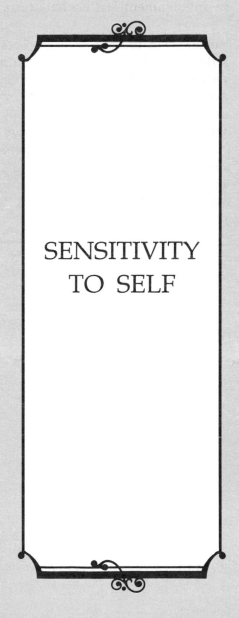

SENSITIVITY TO SELF

ONE

Unexpected Wisdom

We live in hard, cynical times that place little, if any, value on sensitivity to self, others, or God. This is depressing and dangerous not only for us, but also for those who follow and model themselves after us. As the poet Maya Angelou once noted in a presentation on evil: "There is nothing so tragic as a young cynic. Because a young cynic goes from *knowing* nothing to *believing* nothing."[1]

Now more than ever before, when faced with darkness and a desire to give up and pull back, we need to have the courage to embrace a new, sensitive attitude. Rather than running away from reality, no matter how unpleasant it might seem, we must be willing to stand honestly before ourselves, others, and God to see people and events as they truly are. If we don't, our life will continue to be superficial and fragmented, torn by worries, induced needs, and needless confusion.

We must be willing to see not only the good, but also the bad. We must embrace fully not only our talents, but also our limitations, not only our life but even our mortality. This is essential for ourselves and for those who follow us.

As Erik Erikson, the famous developmental psychologist, pointed out in his classic work *Children and Society*: "Healthy children will not fear life if their elders have integrity enough not to fear death."[2] In appreciating our own selves *as we truly are* we can model for others the possibilities which can arise for them as well.

This is by no means a new lesson. It is one known through the ages by spiritual figures and in contemporary society by persons in the fields of psychological healing. As I have noted elsewhere:

> A significant turning point in therapy or counseling arrives when the individual seeking help is able to grasp the following, simple, seemingly paradoxical reality:

> When we truly accept our limits, the opportunity for personal growth and development is almost limitless.

> Prior to achieving this insight, energy is wasted on running away from the self, or running to another image of self. We fear being ourselves and lack the necessary trust in God for personal evolution to take place. Therefore, running in confusion we fail to take the special place in community that creation has destined for us.

> I guess this is not surprising because we are constantly bombarded with the message that we should be someone or something else. ... There is little call for people to fulfill their destiny, and much energy (and money!) is expended on convincing them to avoid it at all costs.[3]

As must be obvious, embracing the truth in all its forms is imperative, but it is easier said than done. Many of us seem to have a deeply felt desire to live honestly and sensitively. Yet, despite a high level of motivation in this area, we still often fail in our efforts to experience life directly in a truthful, unvarnished way. The reality we must face again and again is: motivation is good ... but it is not enough! Charles Kettering, an American engineer and inventor expressed this sentiment accurately and bluntly when he said: "You can be sincere ... and still be stupid!"

And so, as important as motivation is, we need more than motivation to sensitively experience ourselves and the world in which we live, to live lives that are full and strong. If we are to be successful we must also know the right kind of effort to make—an effort that includes embracing a radically new attitude and living out of a more honest identity. One way this can be accomplished more easily is through a deep appreciation of the process of unlearning, so that relearning and responding in new creative ways can become really possible.

Unlearning

People are often concerned about the negative impact of their ignorance. They feel it is what they don't know that will hurt them and this of course is true, to a certain extent. However, I believe that an even more subtle insidious danger than ignorance is what we think we already know but actually don't. True sensitivity and real wisdom begin with recognizing this fact.

At times we tend to be so "hard-hearted" that even when presented with contrary information, we "dig in our heels" and hold onto our opinions rather than being open enough to let in new information that may prove us wrong. I think the following story by Anthony de Mello illustrates this point well. A woman suddenly stops a man walking down the street and says:

"Henry, I am so happy to see you after all these years! My, how you have changed."

"I remember you as being tall and you seem so much shorter now."

"You used to have a pale complexion and it is really so ruddy now."

"Good grief how you have changed in five years!"

Finally, the man got a chance to interject: "But my name isn't Henry!"

To which the persistent woman calmly responded: "Oh, so you changed your name too!"[4]

All through the history of the human race we have heard stories of people being asked to let go, unlearn, reform, renew, and accept an identity that is more in line with who they could become rather than who they have settled for being because of the presence of anxiety or ignorance. For instance, in the book of Genesis in the Hebrew scriptures we see how Abram is called to let go of the identity he had in order to become open to the person he could and should be (Abraham). Likewise, his wife Sarai is asked to let go of her limited sense of self to become Sarah, a woman filled with new potential.

Like them and others throughout history, we are now called to unlearn much of what we have absorbed that is untrue about ourselves and others so we can have an attitude of sensitivity. This will allow us to be open to new realities and new possibilities, and to find our own true name and identity. We can then model this for others so they can also be empowered to see and take their places of dignity in the world. There is so much blocking us from this, and some of these psychological and spiritual obstacles are unfortunately very vague and often subtle.

Uncovering Subtle Styles of Defense

For years, there has been a movement afoot in both psychology and spirituality to release people from the chains of unreasonable guilt and undeserved shame. (Guilt is: "I made a mistake." Shame is: "I am a mistake.")

This has been a very helpful undertaking and there is still much work which needs to be done in this area. However, as with every good movement, there have been some problematic aspects of it. One of them is that in the process of trying to do those things necessary for developing self-esteem, we may have also ignored the styles of defensiveness in us which ultimately prevent both growth and insight.

Such subtle defensiveness can be referred to as "characterological" in nature, and may be best understood by viewing what psychologists have uncovered from working with persons who have personality styles that are inappropriate yet quite ingrained. Persons in these categories are very difficult to treat because they believe that there is nothing wrong with them. In their mind it is the world which needs to change!

They have ingrained, lifelong personality styles of dealing with their lives and the world which they don't find uncomfortable in themselves, but which cause others problems (which in turn may make life tough for them when people react in a negative fashion.) This is very unlike persons suffering the disorder we used to refer to as "neurotic." Persons in this category are well aware of their own problems and are distressed over them.

Consequently, real care needs to be taken with persons in the characterological category. The therapist must not assume that the behavior presented is causing the person inner turmoil and that is why he or she wishes to change it. In addition, one must carefully work to show the person that he or she will have to pay the price if this type of destructive behavior continues—even though it might not be seen in this light at this point.

To illustrate this,[5] let me cite the case of a young woman in her twenties who came in for treatment at the urging of her father. Once she had been greeted and I made sure I had some basic identifying data, I asked her to explain what I could do for her.

She launched into a story of how she had begun college this past fall. She said that as a freshman she tended to socialize with sophomores, drank a great deal, went to parties all the time, let her studies fall down, and almost failed out of school. Then, in the next semester she said she did get expelled for breaking a number of the rules, rarely showing up for class, and having all F grades in her courses. Because of this her parents lost thousands of dollars in tuition for the second semester.

When she returned home, she continued her extreme "social" life with bouts of heavy drinking and wild hours. Late one night, after her parents were in bed, she even brought the young man she was with that evening home with her and they went to bed together in her room. She said they planned to wake up early so as not to get caught, but since they both had so much to drink, they overslept. In the morning her mother came down and upon finding her in bed with this man, became furious, chasing her around the house.

Having told me this story, she sat back waiting for my response. During the telling of the story, when I looked at her face, I didn't see any sense of remorse. Instead there was a general relaxed demeanor interspersed with smiles and light laughter.

Given this, I looked at her and gently said: "It sounds like you have been having quite a good time." She seemed startled, perhaps because of the previous disapproving responses she had received from her family, and said: "Excuse me?"

I said: "It seems like you have been having a lot of fun, a generally wonderful time. Is that not so?"

She finally collected herself and said: "Well, er, yes."

I then replied: "Well we don't treat that here."

After a pause, she replied: "But don't you realize that because of all of this the ceiling is falling in on my head at home?"

"Ah," I responded, "Now, that kind of problem we do treat."

What I was trying to do was not get caught in the trap of responding to her as others had mistakenly done. One of the roles of the therapist is to be a different person to the patient. By doing this it is possible to break through the normal crust of denial and avoidance, name the behavior for what it is, and then look at more productive alternatives.

This illustration is especially relevant here because it shines a light on the fact that a style of interaction which is beyond our level of awareness can be very destructive. In addition, it is also important for us to recognize here that all of us have unproductive characterological styles which, while maybe not as extreme as in the above case, can be just as hidden and quietly destructive to the sensitive way we wish to live and interact with others.

Several brief examples from my own life might help illustrate this point. One happened a long time ago when I was in my twenties. I was having a conflict with a close friend. As we were talking about it, he said to me: "You really are hung up on competition. It is probably due to the fact that you are the youngest of three boys. You really ought to look more closely at your relationship with your brothers, now and when you were growing up."

Upon hearing this, I naturally wanted to deny it and I did at the time. But one of the thoughts I also had about the person telling me this—no doubt for defensive reasons—was: "Why don't you recognize how competition with your own brother is also affecting our relationship and stop acting like it is just my problem!"

As I look back now, I realize that we were both engaged in denial. Both of us were blind to a block in our lives. The helper was as blind as I, and because of it our relationship was blocked from developing any further.

Another encounter with a similar theme occurred when I was in my thirties. I was trying to help someone see how an unproductive style in her life was causing problems and prompting people to speak ill of her behind her back. This time I was in the helping role—or at least I thought so.

Her style was centered on success. She manipulated people to this end and had a reputation of being "slick," even though the ministry she was doing had a positive impact on the leadership of her denomination.

After speaking with her on the phone, we arranged a meeting. I had a hard time trying to think of how to help her face this without forsaking the good she was doing. I also didn't want to cause deep wounds, or make her feel like I was saying she was a bad person—far from the truth. In reality, this person was actually doing many good things at the time, but my feeling was she needed to review her motivations if her work was to be on a sound spiritual footing and continue to flourish.

However, in bringing up the topic I was awkward, too direct, and emotional. As a result, in response to my intervention, she kept asking for specific instances of the problem we were talking about. When I tried to point them out, she had "reasons" for each action and would minimize or rationalize my comments away.

After ten minutes or so, I could see she was already on the defensive because I had been so awkward with her. In addition, I was finding it hard to show her that it wasn't her specific actions (the "lyrics" of her life) but the process (the "music" of her life) that was causing difficulties. In other words, her manipulative acts each taken separately were inconsequential. Added together though, they comprised a way of deception, so subtle yet comprehensive, that she couldn't see the negative impact of her style on others or the reactions people were having in response to the way she was unconsciously using them.

At any rate, while I was stumbling around trying to be of help somehow, she finally caught me up short by interrupting me with the statement: "When you first brought this up to me I thought about your comments. Then I spoke to people whom you know and they concurred that *you* have many of the very faults with which you are confronting me."

At first I passed off her comments as defensive (which would be natural for her to do since I was perceived as attacking her). But then the stark truths in her statements struck like a lightning bolt. Rather than my being a prophet for her, she was a prophet for me. I was in no position to help her remove the "splinter" in her eye while there was a "log" in my own preventing me from growing. Someone else who was more integrated in this area and thus more gentle and holy would have to serve as her prophet.

She had helped me see more than ever before what it means to be someone who is so wrapped up in his image and desires for success that he misses his own problems while seeing those of others so clearly. She was so right. I was indicting her for problems that I had myself and even though my observations were probably correct based on the number of comments people had shared with me about her, since I had similar issues I should have been the last person to try to help her! My motivations in reaching out to her were far from pure.

The final illustration seems a bit more subtle to me, at least. I'd like to think so because it took me so many years to achieve a more complete understanding of what was going on in myself during a long series of interactions with a friend.

For years a friend's ambivalence about taking out time to reflect and pray drove me absolutely crazy. We would sit together, talk about how he might take out time to center himself so his life would be more fruitful and less like a confused marathon, and the result would always be the same in the end ... little or no action.

I felt very conscious of his problem. Often, even when he didn't ask me for advice, I would sit him down and pontificate. (It is a testament to his charity that he didn't once tell me to jump in a lake and stop being so intrusive!)

Finally, one evening when I was thinking about him because he was going to come over for dinner, I thought once more about his ambivalence and my preoccupation with it. However, this time I reflected on why I got so upset about his inability to act. Other things about him didn't upset me. Why this? Why was I making myself so upset over his behavior?

Then, I was graced with an insight. I realized that what was really upsetting for me was something about his apparently impregnable style. It wasn't that he wouldn't take out the time to sit still, reflect, and pray but would instead rush around, simultaneously complaining that all his free time was slipping through his hands. That was a psychologically and spiritually blind alley for me. The real problem for me was that although he knew he had to change, it seemed like he couldn't! He would talk about change and even protest he was changing. But in reality he continued to be in a whirlwind.

This was like a mirror for me. I finally realized that at some preconscious level, I had the fear: "If he can't change in these areas and really believes he is making progress when he is not, then there are ways I can't change and am deluding myself about my so-called 'progress' too." I wanted to change him as a way of proving that I could change too. My so-called "generous" motives really were at heart self-serving, more tied to my own problems than to his.

As a matter of fact, he might be comfortable with his style of ambivalence and I should mind my own business and leave him alone until he asked for some way out of this pattern. (And, even at that point one has to be careful because some people will project their ambivalence onto others, try to get them to take a position, try it, and if it fails blame the helper rather than take responsibility themselves.)

This experience shed a light over a host of my own behaviors as well as the hopes that I had for others; things like: I wish this or that person would pray more, be more grateful and less angry, not drink so much, be less scattered or selfish, not try to monopolize others, be more reflective, not be so busy while claiming he wasn't, and on and on. I needed to look more closely at why I needed so badly for others to behave as I wanted them to in certain situations. While some of my motivations were good and my observations might have been correct to some extent, much of my motivation was tied to my own immaturities and problems.

The psychological and spiritual levy was temporarily broken and the muddy water just kept on flooding me with personal flaws and/or addictions. But with the onslaught of psychological "dirt" quite surprisingly there also came a bit more freedom. I was freed from tyrannizing others to such a degree and freed from worrying so much about my own image.

After seeing all of this (as well as knowing in my heart that there were no doubt many persons in my life who also saw I had these problems, but had the tact not to say it directly to me), I thought: How could I ever prop up an image of myself as a model of spiritual success? Or more importantly: Why would I ever want to? The freedom that came with this insight was pure grace; something certainly to be grateful for and to try not to forget. As Margaret Mitchell, author of *Gone with the Wind*, once said: "Until you've lost your reputation, you never realize what a burden it was or what freedom really is."[6]

Yet, even after recognizing the subtlety of only a few of my own characterological (ingrained and personally unrecognizable) defenses, I knew I was just seeing the tip of the iceberg. There was still so much more that I didn't see or know. However, I felt an attitude shift and some hope.

I was caught in a good paradox. On one level, I somehow recognized that God loved me and on the other hand, I began to appreciate the reality that everyone in my life who has said negative things about me—no matter how noble or poor their motivations might have been—was correct to some extent and could be my teacher if I were willing to be taught. And this "if" would hinge on whether or not I could appreciate the great rewards this information could provide for me.

Also, since I feel I am a realist, I know how elusive true humility is for me and how difficult it would be for me to live my life steeped in a real openness to the truth rather than one that was merely proclaimed to be so. The following wonderful Hasidic story humorously points to this difficulty:

> There was once a famous rabbi. One day he was standing inside his synagogue with his arms stretched to the heavens loudly saying: "God I am nothing! Absolutely nothing!"

Seeing this, his cantor joined him and standing next to him also raised his arms to the heavens and cried: "God I am nothing! Absolutely nothing!"

Finally, a maintenance man who happened by saw the two of them making their declarations and he went and stood next to them as well and also shouted out: "God I am nothing! Absolutely nothing!"

At which point, the rabbi turned to the cantor, made a face, and said: "Look who thinks he's nothing!"[7]

The obvious lesson: humility and true spiritual sensitivity are elusive graces—even when we think they are what we seek. However, to give up the quest to embrace the truth because of the natural difficulty all of us have to see ourselves in an unvarnished way is unacceptable. We must persist, no matter what, if we wish to enter into the peace that is lying underneath the pain that self-discovery sometimes initially brings with it.

But part of this persistence is the willingness to ask honest, yet sometimes initially painful questions, such as:

1) What is the style I feel people find most wonderful in me and when do I "trip over" it? (In other words, if I am outgoing, vital and gregarious, when do I monopolize situations, avoid listening, or not allow others to share their talents?)

2) What is the one comment I hate to hear about myself? What truth is there in such a comment?

3) When am I most judgmental of myself and others? How do I understand such a judgmental attitude?

4) What are the ways I am avoiding or refusing the love that is already around me?

5) What makes me the most anxious, stressful, and angry? And, in addition to the possibly good reasons for such reactions, what are some of the immature ones?

6) Who is the person I dislike or can't seem to get along with in most situations? What is this person inadvertently teaching me about myself that I don't want to admit?

When we acknowledge, enter, and embrace what the psychiatrist Carl Jung referred to as "our shadow" (which contains many hidden negative feelings, impulses, and motivations that counterbalance much of our overt positive emotions and attitudes), the possibilities to discover new creative elements in our personality and to open up new avenues for personal growth come to light. The following illustration by Robert Johnson exemplifies this in a unique and wonderful way:

> I recently heard about a couple who had the good sense to call upon the shadow in a wedding ceremony. The night before their marriage, they held a ritual where they made their "shadow vows." The groom said, "I will give you an identity and make the world see you as an extension of myself." The bride replied, "I will be compliant and sweet, but underneath I will have the real control. If anything goes wrong, I will take your money and your house." They then drank champagne and laughed heartily at their foibles, knowing that in the course of the marriage, these shadow figures would inevitably come out. They were ahead of the game because they had recognized the shadow and unmasked it.[8]

Unlearning requires then a ruthless willingness to be open to the truth about ourselves and brings with it great rewards in self-knowledge and freedom from being bound up in our defenses or shadow. It also loosens up creative energy to experience ourselves, others, and God in new ways.

However, to be involved in such a process relies heavily on our ability to undertake it while simultaneously being very clear that we are loved and special in the eyes of God. Without this, our self-awareness will slowly turn into self-condemnation and will be a doorway to guilt and shame rather than to knowledge and growth. And so, reviewing this very point at this juncture might be helpful.

Receiving: Sowing the Seeds of Healthy Self-Love

When we think of being a sensitive and compassionate person, one of the first things that comes to mind is giving. This is not very unusual, since every major philosophy and religion emphasizes that to be truly human we must share with others. We must not just be willing to merely talk about being a loving person, we must do something about it.

Isn't this one of the major tenets of the controversial New Testament epistle of James? Simply put, his point is: "Put up or shut up!" He rightly recognizes that we shouldn't claim to be loving people if we are not acting that way. Love is only real in the concrete, or as the Chinese proverb says: "Talk doesn't cook rice."

Yet, the greatest challenge to living a sensitive life may be a real surprise for many of us. The major spiritual challenge is not the willingness to give love. Instead, I believe it is the ability to *receive* love. Otherwise, our giving can become too compulsive, tentative, and conditional. Without having a deep sense of being loved we are not really able to give with a sense of *mitzvah*—giving and expecting nothing in return. Rather, we share with a sense of expectancy. If people don't show gratitude or follow our suggestions (which they rarely do!), we feel let down, hurt, depressed, angry, "used." But if we are continually open to receiving love, we don't worry as much about people's reactions. We simply give and leave it at that. The process is in itself rewarding.

The problem is that if we have not taken steps to unlearn our assumptions, expectations, and demands, and can't let go of our "neediness"—and all this brings with it—we cannot learn simple new ways to receive the love that is already around us. Therefore our true, loving attitude will not last for very long.

We will not feel replenished, and we will become inclined to rely on those whom we reach out to for our restoration—at best a very precarious situation! Being able to appreciate new ways of experiencing love (a relearning process) is essential for those wishing to live a sensitive life. Such a life carries with it a deep sense of meaning, purpose, peace, and perspective.

One problem with such an attitude is that we can often be too stubborn in our designation of what love is for us. I sometimes see this in my patients when I give them some positive feedback. I am a fairly direct person. I always tease people that even though I took the courses "Subtlety 101 and 102" in my doctoral clinical psychology program, I barely passed them. As a result, when I offer a positive comment to someone, I truly mean it, and have illustrations and evidence to support it. Despite this, the look on their faces in response to such comments often seems to belie one of the following statements: "Oh, psychologists are supposed to say nice things like that;" or, "If he really knew me, he wouldn't say such things;" or (the one I really like), "If he really knows me and likes me, what does that say about him!!" It's like the old joke, who would want to join a club that would accept me?

We also dismiss the love in our environment in other truly foolish ways without recognizing our actions for what they are. For instance, once I was visiting another country to lead a retreat and I noticed an encounter between two lay missionaries who hadn't seen each other in six months. The man was standing there and a young smiling woman ran up to him virtually bursting with good cheer. She hugged him and said how great it was to see him.

Later in the day I had the chance to share with the man that I had seen the meeting and commented about how affirming it must have been for him to be greeted in that way. He responded: "Oh, she treats everyone like that," dismissing this experience of love as unimportant.

This is, of course, totally ridiculous. Certainly, we wouldn't go to the Bahamas and walk out onto the beach on a beautiful day and say to the friend with us: "Oh, this is no good; the sun is shining on everybody here. Let's go back indoors." Yet, we do the same thing every day with wonderful people who are good to us.

Sensitivity, in terms of the trait of "reception," calls us to be more open to the positive reactions of others, to be more tolerant with ourselves and others, and to be freer to see how our destructive games limit our ability to receive—and therefore to give—love.

I truly believe that Madonna Kohlbenschlag has it right when she says in her book *Lost in the Land of Oz* that "The refusal to relate is the sin of our times."[9] But maybe this is because we have not felt loved enough to do so, or because we have not seen the unconscious ways we avoid, deny, minimize, ignore, or distort the love that is really already there for us.

The challenge to love is certainly matched by our challenge to see where we are not finding the love that is there. This keystone to self-esteem is so important because it allows us to be more honest in the way we view ourselves and others. With it we become free to subsequently view our faults in an unblemished way without also condemning ourselves in the process. We are able to see people for who they are now and who they could become without judging them inferior because of our hidden needs and secret expectations.

The ability to receive love then is a very important element in leading the sensitive life and it sets the stage for us to see our own faults with a sense of inquisitiveness rather than self-condemnation. It also frees us up to see God in so many ways in our life, to take "side-trips" into wisdom each day.

"Side-Trips" into Wisdom

Just prior to their 1993 elections I was invited into Cambodia to do a workshop on stress for English-speaking NGOs (Non-Governmental Officials) from the international community. Professionals constantly working with persons suffering from stress, physical and psychological trauma, anxiety, sexual/physical abuse, and depression are prone to difficulties themselves and this was a chance to help these professionals keep their emotional flame alive while extending their warmth to others.

They were from the United States, Canada, France, Ethiopia, Malta, Japan, Thailand, Cambodia, and several other countries. These persons were working closely with the Khmer people of Cambodia to help them rebuild their nation after a long period of terror during the reign of Pol Pot. They included professionals in psychiatry, ministry, education, relief work, psychology, and general medicine. When I got to know them I found them to be really amazing people.

In Cambodia, I expected that "vicarious posttraumatic stress," a specific form of secondary stress, would especially be a problem among helping professionals, because so many people in Cambodia had undergone terror, anxiety, and trauma at the hands of the Khmer Rouge regime. And so, I expected that those who worked with them had to be affected in a similar way as well.

As is my custom when I visit a new setting, I try to experience in some small but symbolic way what the people are going through who work there. In this case, to get a sense of the terror of the times and to get a feeling as to what had gone on in Cambodia, I arranged to visit both "the Killing Fields" and Tuol Sleng (a high school which had been turned into a torture chamber by the Khmer Rouge).

In visiting the Killing Fields, I was stunned by the monument which contained rows and rows of skulls of some of the one and a half million victims who died during the totalitarian rule. I walked on the bits of bones and pieces of shirts and pants that still littered the ground and witnessed the leg and arm bones which protruded from places in the ground. They were left there in gaping holes which marked the exhumation of at least some of the torture victims.

Following the visit to the Killing Fields I then went to see Tuol Sleng, a large makeshift prison covered with a barbed wire mesh so those captive there could not jump and commit suicide during their excruciatingly painful interrogations. Tuol Sleng was an especially horrible place, to say the least. (One of the drivers could not even enter the grounds because he once was a student there when it was a high school and when it became a prison, both his parents had been tortured and killed there.)

As I walked the cramped dark corridors and visited the torture rooms that were still stained with blood, I could not help but take in the horror of what had happened. I wondered "How could the people who hadn't died during this period go on? How could those who had to witness all of this terror and torture continue to survive psychologically and spiritually?"

After leaving both settings, I knew that there was something in the visit to these two sites that would give special meaning to my trip and that these two "highlights" would mark me for the future. However, as poignant as they were, two other side-trips in wisdom and faith raised my sensitivity to a lesson that may have been even more important yet possibly missed if my heart hadn't been graced by an openness at the time.

The first was in my own hotel. During my stay in a little place operated by Khmers (the name for the people of Cambodia) who had returned from France after the downfall of the Khmer Rouge government, I had the pleasure of interacting with the staff each day.

One of them frequently served as receptionist at the desk and also as supervisor for others who were working on the main floor. She was impressive not only because of her mastery of several languages but also because of her outgoing, warm, cheerful attitude.

On one occasion early in my stay I had wanted to ask her a question about one of the services in the hotel and I approached the desk. Since the area surrounding it was carpeted and she was busy working on some administrative task, she didn't hear or see me coming. When she finally looked up she was startled. The startle reaction was not a normal gasp of surprise but a sharp intake of air and an expression on her face of real fear and horror. It was a typical startle reaction for someone who was suffering from a posttraumatic stress disorder (PTSD). It was not unusual since so many people were threatened, raped, tortured, and terrorized during the Pol Pot regime and she was just old enough to have been a small, impressionable child during that time.

Although I knew this and should have expected it, I was taken aback by the look on her face. Even though I had been a psychologist and worked in hospitals as well as private practice for a long time, and also served in the Marine Corps where I experienced many types of difficult situations and people, the look of pure terror on her face had a deep impact on me. It reminded me of the look on my mother's face when I told her that my father had just died and she tried to comprehend that she would never see him again.

There was a basic lesson here for me. The pain some people must endure in living their simple lives is beyond belief. Their courage can add meaning not only to their lives but to ours if we have the eyes to see it, the ears to hear it, and the heart to embrace it. Yet, too often we want to run away from the necessary pain in our own lives and in the lives of others. The result of this is a life of denial and hidden anxiety. We live in constant fear of losing comfort, security, one's image in the eyes of others, or the illusory control we believe we have over life. At such times peace is beyond our reach and what we may mistake for pure joy is a fleeting sense of happiness that in its absence leaves us lonely, bored, and adrift waiting for the next "fix" of fun.

The second encounter was on my first Sunday in Cambodia. On that day I was invited to drive outside the city of Phnom Penh to visit a village of ethnic Vietnamese who had lived peacefully in Cambodia for generations along the Mekong River. When we arrived we were given a choice to stay on one side of the river or to take a small boat across to visit a village on the other side where we could also attend a liturgy. The village had recently had a series of mysterious house-burnings that were tentatively attributed to the Khmer Rouge who, although situated in the north, tended to make incursions throughout the country.

I chose to go across the river. Upon my arrival I met a man who had been a victim of the house-burnings. He had only the clothes he was wearing. All else had been lost.

As he showed us the remnants of his house and the ashes of some of the others which had been burned, I looked around and saw that many of his fellow Vietnamese, because of their fear, had literally picked up their houses, loaded them into their boats piece by piece, and left to return to Vietnam—a "home" some of them had never lived in or possibly even seen before this trip. Of the original 570 homes, only 70 remained. And this man and his family were among them.

In walking through the village the anguish on his face struck me. Still, as we moved through the village, I noticed someone else as well. As I walked along, a young girl of about eight kept bumping into me. Finally I realized (people like me can be really dense!) that she wanted me to take her hand. I finally did and we walked together until we reached the church for liturgy.

After liturgy and a short lunch with the village elders in a lean-to like structure which served as a sacristy, we proceeded back to the boat to cross the river again. This time both the man whose house had been burned and the little girl (who turned out to be his daughter) came with us. She sat next to me in the boat, holding onto my hand, and we shared the time in silence with her father and the others while re-crossing the river back to the other side.

I hope I'll never forget the experience of their presence with me in the boat. The man's face showed anguish yet commitment. The young girl's face showed hope. Being with the both of them at one time and feeling the emotions of a special day (as well as the emotions engendered by the encounter with the traumatized young hotel-clerk) broke through the psychological and social crust of my understanding of life in a way that even the Killing Fields and Tuol Sleng—as important and dramatic as these experiences were—could not. Maybe the difference was the personal contact.

I knew at the core of my being that real life, *the sensitive life*, must contain by its very nature both the anguish of painful realities and the hope of what still can come to fruition. This insight helped me look at my life and others in a very different way. I knew at a deeper level that one couldn't escape the dire realities we all must face if we wish to be alive rather than die slowly, hidden under a psychological shroud of denial and avoidance. Dorothee Soelle, speaking about suffering, has distinguished two kinds of suffering: unnecessary and necessary. Her advice was simple (once one made a discernment as to which suffering it was): Avoid the unnecessary sufferings in life and face the necessary ones.[10]

However, I learned another lesson of possibly equal importance: when one is suffering one must also remember the important reality of hope. Hope isn't simply believing that things will go well because one is a good person who deserves such rewards. Instead, hope is an attitude of living which makes one seek and find new possibilities because of an attitude of trust. As Vaclav Havel, the poet-leader of the Czech Republic, recognizes:

> Hope is an orientation of the spirit, an orientation of the heart. It is not the conviction that something will turn out well, but the certainty that something makes sense, regardless of how it turns out.[11]

I guess a good example of this can be seen in some of the people who are involved in relief work throughout the world. In an interview on public radio, Dr. Collins, a physician in Somalia, commented on our reaction to the starving people of Somalia. While people who saw them on TV felt despair, those who met them, those who knew them as more than anonymous faces, had a different experience. Like those who saw the horror of starvation on television, they felt the pain—maybe they even experienced more pain—but they also felt something else, something very significant. It was reflected in one comment he made during the interview when he said: "You can't give up hope when you are making friends."

At a very basic level the young girl I travelled with across the Mekong River had a sense of trust. She had inherited the deep faith of her family and the community of Vietnamese people who had faced adversity generation after generation. She also had trusted us, the priests who had been coming week after week to minister to her people and the persons the priests had brought with them on this trip. Fortunately for me I was one of them. I could learn from them all if only I had the eyes to see.

The man in his anguish, like the traumatized clerk, still had the ability to trust. They knew they had to persevere, and they did. Could I see this and learn too? The little girl whose home was burned down also had a lesson to teach—the fresh continuance of hope. Would I accept this, learn from it, and be able to maintain perspective in my life as well? Would I continue to be sensitive to the people and lessons that each day held for me, or would I try to run away, psychologically and spiritually, in search of security and comfort and then call it peace?

With sensitivity to others, the deep yearnings within me and to the ongoing presence of God in the world in so many different places, life could be so much different, so much more. It is certainly something worth seeking. The pearl of great price always is, isn't it?

I knew, in that moment of insight in Cambodia, where the spiritual action was. I knew where life really dwelt. It didn't matter whether I experienced pain or joy, or maybe both. What did matter was whether I sought to dwell in, and be sensitive to, the Truth. I knew, at some level, maybe in some way for the first time, how surely it would set me free. The motivation in me was there, and having such a desire to unlearn and relearn certainly seemed to be an important first step.

When we possess a sacred curiosity and an objectivity that allows us to see things more clearly and without passion, we are able to respond with a new sense of spontaneity. There is a willingness to take risks in relationships—not just with others, but with our view of nature, material things, and especially our view of ourselves and God!

We no longer need be on a seesaw of comfortable complacency balanced by occasional, abrupt, rash acts of desperation because we fear that life is slipping through our hands. With this new interest in unlearning, relearning, and responding to life in a new way, it may become really possible to grasp something that may have been elusive or incomprehensible to us up to this point. When sensitivity is pure and real it can actually open us up to life in a way that daily mysticism can become a natural way of living rather than merely a subject of occasional fantasy. And, it is to this topic that we shall turn next.

TWO

Daily
Mysticism

Being sensitive to oneself goes hand in hand with developing a nurturing sensitive self who is not only open to greater self-understanding, but also to sensing the world in new, remarkable ways. Unfortunately though, preconceived notions are like a screen between us and the world. As the well-known Indian mystic Krishnamurti once observed: "We hardly ever listen to the sound of a dog's bark, or the cry of a child, or the laughter of a man as he passes by. We separate ourselves from everything, and then from this isolation look and listen to all things."[1]

Anthony de Mello went on to echo and expand upon this theme when he wrote:

> The royal road to mysticism and to reality ... passes through the world of actions that are enjoyed in and for themselves without an eye to success or to gain. ... The moment you touch this reality, you will know what freedom and love are.[2]

We think we see but often really see very little; believe we listen yet only hear a small portion; have insight and understanding but are bound by what we knew beforehand.

As was mentioned in the previous chapter, to really appreciate the world before us and in us in a sensitive, fresh way, the processes of unlearning and relearning must take on a new priority. Then a radically new sensitivity, what I believe can be referred to as "daily mysticism," becomes possible. And maybe the best way this can happen is if we begin to see the import of five key elements of this daily mysticism:

1. Letting go,

2. Being in the now,

3. Appreciating the value of experiencing deep gratitude,

4. Knowing the impact of having a greater openness to passion and awe,

5. Seeking and maintaining a simple sense of perspective.

1. Letting Go ... or Is It, "Being With"?

In visiting one of the Canadian maritime provinces, I remember walking along the harbor with a friend. As we passed a dry dock, I noticed they were using a special device to clean the barnacles off the hull in preparation for repainting.

I indicated to my friend that it was nice that they were doing this and that it would really be pleasant to look at the ship once they were done. The implication left hanging in the air was that the company must be going through all this expense to make people like me feel good. In response, my friend gave me a look that said: "Were you born yesterday?"

He pointed out that the shipping company had discovered that it was cheaper to go through this whole process rather than to pay the cost incurred by the ship being slowed down due to the crustacean material that adheres itself to the hull of the ship over the course of a long journey from the oil fields to the refineries. They put out the effort and money to clean off the barnacles and use a barnacle-resistant paint not for aesthetics, but for the cost benefit.

Isn't this also the case in our letting go of the unfinished psychological business that is blinding, slowing us down, or holding us back? Instead, due to long-term hurts or "neediness" this lesson is frequently not learned. Thus, we are silently distracted from and therefore unable to be sensitive to what is important and good in our lives now.

Most of us seem to be predisposed to keep investing good energy in an effort to make a bad experience better. For instance, I have never been known for my financial acumen. A number of years ago I bought 5,000 shares of a particular over-the-counter stock for $1.00 share. After a period of time I called the stock broker and asked what it was worth. He said: $8.24 and I responded excitedly: "You mean a share?" "No," he responded, "the whole lot."

After I got over the shock of learning about my financial loss, I asked him what I should do. He halfheartedly suggested I might consider buying more so I could even off the price-per-share cost of the original purchase. (To show you how bright I am, I even spent ten seconds thinking that it might be a good idea!)

Although the thought of doing what the broker suggested is ludicrous, this seems to be what many of us do in life when confronted with past interpersonal problems and the potential of present possibilities. For instance, years ago a Catholic religious sister from Eastern Europe who saw me in therapy had a very bad time of it during the first twenty years in her religious order. She couldn't seem to let go of her feelings of bitterness.

She spent the first three sessions with me telling me about the difficulties she had experienced through her early years up to the present. As the fourth session began, she was going to go over the same ground again. I interrupted her and said: "I believe you. I don't think you are making it up."

Since we had formed the beginning of a fairly good relationship, I teased her: "I have enough. Type it up and we will send it to your mother general."

She looked at me in a funny way, rightly suspecting I was kidding her, and said: "Whatever for?"

"So we can get an official apology, of course!"

She laughed and said: "Oh yeh, a real chance that will happen."

So, I persisted along the same track: "Well, how about this then? You will get your reward for this pain in heaven."

To which she responded: "I am not going to buy that I can tell you."

"Well" I teased, "You are a nun, so I thought I would at least try!" and then we both laughed.

Finally, with a serious note in my voice and on my face I said: "Well, this leaves us with only two options. You can hold onto this pain and wait for the Parousia (second coming of Christ) and your reward, or you can let go, benefit from what you have learned, and be open to the joyful possibilities of the rest of your life."

Although she wanted desperately to let go, she left therapy and went off to minister in the southwest, still holding onto her past pain and hurt. This is sad, but all of us, I'm afraid, reflect this person in more subtle and less dramatic ways. The roots of hurt often seed a demanding and needy nature, and we don't recognize it.

Even when people seem to know that their excessive demands turn people off, there is an innate hesitation to let go of the past because they feel that somehow magically they should get rewarded for what they didn't get as children, youths, or earlier in life. The reality in life, though, is that the world is not a just place. Yet there is love in the world if we are willing to recognize and seek it in creative, open ways.

Neediness

Anxiety and learned neediness can also prevent people from letting go of unfinished business and destructive lifestyles. A good way to understand this is to image yourself as a young child who opens the refrigerator after breakfast and sees a beautiful piece of Key lime pie. You know you are full and wouldn't enjoy it now, but look forward to having it later while watching TV. As the time nears 8:00 p.m. and your favorite show is about to come on TV, you go to the refrigerator to get out the pie you have been thinking about all day long. But when you open the refrigerator, it is gone! Someone has already eaten it.

Well, what is the solution to this problem? Is it to pout over it? To berate oneself for not having eaten it before? Or, is it to promise oneself to eat pie when we see it even if we are not hungry, even if it may overfill and make us uncomfortable?

Even though these kinds of solutions don't seem sensible, people who have had emotional deprivation earlier in life or hurts during their adolescence and young adulthood often do emotionally respond as adults in such unusual ways. Instead of being able to let go of their neediness and to sensitively enjoy each day in a way that avoids control, manipulation, or unrealistic expectations of others—in short, to make the most of what they have now—the opposite occurs. But instead of a stomachache because of eating too much pie, they get heartache. Anxiety about interpersonal loss, anger over real or perceived hurts, and an insensitive relational style based on smothering or rigidity with respect to others dominates them.

Surfacing Hurts and Injustices

Letting go also requires us to surface, recognize, and release the hurts we have received in life. When we feel upset over something we must take out the time at some point in the day to reflect on our negative feelings. We need to ask ourselves: "What am I really reacting to in such a strong fashion?" Then once we recognize what the source(s) of the upset is, then we should allow our emotions to be expressed about it—even if this means doing it safely in the privacy of our own room or with a close friend. Although it may seem silly, having a friend hold a pillow which we hit while expressing our anger is a great deal more productive than burying our upset or suddenly exploding inappropriately at a time or in a place we wish we hadn't.

To varnish over negative occurrences does nothing but push them down further in the psyche where they sit and act without our awareness. They must be allowed to rise and be open to examination and healing.

It is natural to be angry and hurt over mistreatment by the people in our lives. It's like grabbing a hot poker—it would be foolish not to yell, and yell loudly. Still, once we have seen the sadness and the time is right, we must let go and move on in life. In the case of sexual abuse the process may take years and require patience on the part of both the victim and those supporting her/him. Certainly, not to do so would be as foolish as holding onto a hot poker while yelling. It just doesn't make any sense.

Whether we like it or not, in the end we are the ones who have the main responsibility for ourselves and whether we can live a truly sensitive adult life which includes letting go and facing life as it is. As reality therapists tell us, we must be willing to recognize, understand, accept, and live within the "givens." Or, as Kahlil Gibran wrote in his famous work *Sand and Foam*: "We choose our joys and sorrows long before we experience them."[3]

The fact that we are provided with limits and "givens" in our life is a reality. To deny such constraints would be "Pollyanna" thinking. Still, despite these constraints, there is much before us, both in reality and in potential, which we are missing because of our unwillingness to let go. I think Dag Hammarskjold in his journal *Markings* was correct when he said: "We are not permitted to choose the frame of our destiny. But what we put into it is ours."[4]

Thomas Merton also recognized this in the following passage from his novel *My Argument with the Gestapo*:

> If you want to identify me, ask me not where I live, or what I like to eat, or how I comb my hair, but ask me what I am living for, in detail, and ask me what

I think is keeping me from living fully for the thing I want to live for.[5]

Surfacing and recognizing our hurts are important first steps. Releasing them is quite another matter! People often say to me: "I'd love to let go but I can't seem to do it. Can you suggest a way?"

I think this is a fair question. The practical suggestion I offer again and again is: If you can't seem to let go of the hurts, then be with them in a new way. Being with what you can't seem to work through or let go of in a different way may be the best response you can make. Too often we are too "macho" in our approaches, trying to conquer the feelings that we don't like. And when we can't we feel frustrated at our inability to work them through or let them go.

To deal with this I often suggest to people that they make friends with their "shadows," that they sit down and metaphorically put what they can't let go of (a thought or feeling) on the table in front of them and dialogue with it. If we have feelings of insecurity or feel buffeted in some fashion, we can be open to this negative presence in our life instead of trying to ignore or be tyrannized by it.

For instance, if someone invites me to give a talk and then for some reason or other cancels it, my reaction may be: "Oh, I feel rejected. I wonder if I said or did something wrong?" Then I might be tempted to shrug it off even though it still vaguely bothers me. Or, I might be haunted by it and not be able to put it aside. I might also try to deal with it by thinking bad things about the person who was the trigger for this feeling. However, none of these steps are really helpful, nor do they make any psychological or spiritual sense.

On the other hand, if I recognize I have a negative feeling, note that it is similar to ones I have had like that in the past, and am willing to dialogue with it, the negative force can be taken out of it. So, in the example cited above, I could sit down and dialogue with my feeling in the following way:

Oh, so you are here again. I'm not surprised. Everywhere I go you seem to come along with me and wait for something to happen that I don't like. You try to make me feel unnecessary guilt and shame.

Well I am used to you. I know that foolish self-doubt goes with me everywhere I go, but I also know that I am loved and loved deeply by God. I also know that this lack of trust in God's love will always be with me and that I must recognize this as one of my faults. However, I am not going to let this fault stop me.

In the past I used to try to conquer you or hide you from myself. It was like I was trying to lock you outside of the house. But each time you would surface and come back in and I, in my self-condemnation and self-doubt, would give you an inordinately prominent place in the house of my life—the master bedroom, the living room. I'd dote on you and feed you a banquet.

Now I know you are part of me—like the chaff that grows beside the wheat—but I am only going to give you a little attention. Instead of so much room in my life, you will have the attic, and instead of a banquet I will give you only a sandwich, just a little attention.

And each time I give you attention it will be to remind myself that, in the spirit of John 15, I am a friend of God's. In addition, it will help to remind me that I need to recall God's love each day so I don't take the Lord or grace for granted. So, thank you for being here to remind me of my dependence on God. Thank you for reminding me that holiness and perfection are not synonymous. And thank you for sitting here with me to remind me that this incident can help me to learn about myself and the love of God.

Unmasking the Charlatan

The more we can realize that we are a friend of God's, the more we can face our faults, fears, defenses, and enter

into our shadow. When we learn how to befriend our negative feelings and to see beyond them to our true selves, we
discover that we are, at the core, lovable. And in faith we
begin to recognize more and more that God does indeed love
us. And so, unmasking the charlatan in ourselves is important for psychological reasons, but even more important for
spiritual reasons.

Once, when sitting with Trappist Abbot Flavian Burns,
he began to speak about Thomas Merton. He said that Merton was very concerned about seeing the truth about himself.
Abbot Flavian went on to note that when we die, he believes
we will see ourselves in a true light. He said Merton probably
wasn't too surprised by what he saw. However, when most
of us die, we will probably be chagrined at what we see. In
response, I teased him: "Maybe the word 'chagrin' would
aptly fit your response, but I have a feeling a stronger word
will fit me when I die."

There is a Zen saying: "Face reality and unwilled change
will take place." If we are willing to see ourselves as we are
while simultaneously holding onto the fact that we are loved
(and loved deeply) by God, then much effortless change will
become possible.

Often we don't look at ourselves honestly because we
are fearful and anxious at what we will see. The question
we need to ask ourselves is: are we willing to risk seeing
the truth about ourselves? Or, possibly more pointedly:
how much lack of safety can we tolerate in our journey into
self-awareness?

If we don't look at ourselves honestly, much self-
delusion can and will take place. Even if we are well read and
travelled, our world view can still be narrow. Even our good
traits can get overemphasized because of poor motivation.
As Robert Coles pointed out in one of his talks at Loyola
College in the fall of 1993: "Drive and ambition are good; but
they can, as in the case of Napoleon, put us in the middle of
a Russian winter."

2. *Being in the Now*

Just as preoccupations with past hurts and nostalgia can block our sensitivity, so can seeking control by staring ahead into the future. It does this by wasting opportunities for taking responsibility for one's life and living in "the now." Without appreciating the now, much potential appreciation of self, others, and the experiences of life are foregone. Simple daily mysticism and sensitivity to wonder and awe become impossible. Moreover, our actions in "the now" are a microcosm of our whole lives; they provide us with a real sense of the form our whole life will take.

Maybe a good way to understand this is to look at a type of geometry which is intriguing many young scientists—"fractals." The study and explanation of fractals are attributed to a person named Mandelbrot. Through the use of geometry he showed that things seem to look identical at different scales.

For instance, if you look at a mountain and reflect on its shape, you can then successfully find this shape present in the smaller peaks on it. And even if you look at a piece of rock with a magnifying glass or view through a microscope a small section of that rock, you will be able to view a similar basic fractal shape.[6]

The relevance of fractals here is that some people got so excited about them that they applied them to human life. They paralleled a person's day to a week, month, year, and lifetime. What they found was while there were differences (for instance, one day we may be more busy or depressed for some reason), the basic attitude we have toward our day is the attitude we will have toward our lives. Charlotte Gilman recognizes this from a different angle in her journal entitled *The Forerunner*: "Eternity is not something that happens after you are dead. It is going on all the time. We are in it now."[7] Therefore, "the redemption of the now" is one of the greatest steps we can take to live a life of appreciation and wonder, to live the sensitive life.

Being in the now also offers us freedom from anxiety and an opportunity to experience God in refreshing new ways. Many people are not aware that you can't be anxious in the now. It is only when you move into the future without God that you experience anxiety.

Any pain can be experienced without anxiety until we ask how long will it last? Even if you were standing on the tracks in front of an oncoming train, you would have no anxiety until you realized what would happen in the future if you remained there. The now is anxiety free. Being in the now can relieve us of the unnecessary preoccupations and worry about things in the future which may never even happen. Being in the now also helps us to gain enough emotional clarity to plan. While planning is a future-oriented activity done in the now, it is one whose fruits are good, whereas preoccupation just brings us worry and un-needed additional stress. Planning as a now-oriented activity is based on the philosophy of action-and-trust: "I'll do what I can and leave the rest in God's hands."

Spiritually, being in the now is also essential because it is the only place that the living God is present to us. The past may be sacred, the future may hold great graces, but a sensitive encounter with God is in the present moment.

3. A Deep Sense of Gratitude: The Start of a Positive Circle

Just as being in the now helps us to be more sensitive and alert persons, so does a grateful heart. And, in turn, those who tend to be appreciative seem to find even more for which to be grateful when they are present to life rather than bound up in the past or anxiously trying to jump into the future.

One of the main obstacles to a sense of gratitude is bitterness. It blocks us from having a special sensitivity to God's presence in ourselves and in what is going on around us. With an attitude of bitterness it doesn't matter how many potential good things might happen, one is still blocked from reaching one's deep ability to be happy and at peace. As the Jewish proverb goes: "If you are bitter at heart, sugar in the mouth will not help you."

Bitterness prevents us from letting go of hurts so we can welcome good things in our life. A healthy grief gradually leads us to let go and to be open to the new. Depression, on the other hand, moves us in the opposite direction, to hold on to what we have lost. Like depression, bitterness is the result of holding on rather than letting go.

Competition also destroys joyful possibilities of the present. Again, a proverb, this time a German one, would do well for us: "Birds of prey do not sing." By preying on life, we cease to enjoy its innate pleasures in the now.

I used to get a kick out of one of my elderly neighbors. I would be killing myself outside trying to make my yard look good. The healthy part of this was that I enjoyed the exercise and the possibilities to be creative. Yet, like all amateur landscapers, I would compare my outdoor display with the others in the neighborhood. This took some of the joy out of it and sometimes caused me to overdo it physically in an effort to produce what I considered to be good results in a short amount of time. I wanted my yard to be more impressive than their's.

Well, my elderly neighbor would teach me a daily lesson in this regard. Each day he would pass by slowly on his walk and look over the fence and appreciate the work I had done. He would drink it in and enjoy the beauty of it all, and then walk on with his dog.

He wasn't into competition or ownership. It didn't seem to matter to him whether I worked hard or not, whether it was a better display of bushes and flowers than other neighbors or not. It didn't even appear to bother him that I temporarily held title to the land. He enjoyed it as much as I did. As a matter of fact, I think he enjoyed it more!

We miss so much of what life sets before us, and that is sad. We're like people in a room filled with Italian food and we are busy looking for the French food while the food before us gets cold. We need to enjoy the Italian food now (the present gifts in your life) so we'll know how to enjoy the French food later (the future gifts), if and when it's there. Isn't it crazy that most of us are so concerned about how many years we will be on this earth when we're not even living sensitively in the time we have now?

The Wonderful Paradox of Gratefulness

Continuing with the image of dining, I'd like to tell you about two experiences I had which especially brought this point to light for me. A number of years ago I went to a very expensive French restaurant where a meal for one person cost about $75.00. (Thank goodness I wasn't paying for it!) The man at the next table ordered pepper steak—or as they called it, *steak au poivre*. It was one of the most expensive items on the menu. After he was served this *entre* he got into an animated discussion with the woman opposite him and started shoveling his steak down without tasting it. Each time he would take a bite, I would think: "There goes $5.00 untasted and unappreciated."

Last year I had a similar experience with a very different outcome. This time I was at Camden Yards, the home of the Baltimore Orioles baseball team. A man several seats away from me bought a hot dog that cost $3.50. He sat down and prepared to eat it. Unlike the man in the restaurant, he seemed to go through a ritual of attending to his meal. First, he slowly unwrapped it, held it at arms length, looked at it and sighed. Then he slowly put on the mustard and relish. He held it up and sighed again. Then he took a bite, chewed slowly and smiled.

Instead of watching the home team warm up for the game, I was totally taken with this man's ritual. I turned to my wife and said: "If this guy had incense, he would incense that hot dog before eating it."

But what was he doing? He was appreciating a small gift of life. And he was doing it in a way that the man who spent over ten times the amount didn't bother to do. Who was more gifted? The man with the large expense account or the man with a few dollars to spare? Gratefulness not only allows us to appreciate the little things we have, it makes us sensitive to how much more there already is to be grateful for in our lives.

4. A Sense of Passion and Awe

When we can let go in life, appreciate "the now," and have our appreciative senses fed by an attitude of gratitude, then the possibility for experiencing life with a sense of passion and awe becomes real. This is important because awe is at the core of a life of sensitivity. As Nikos Kazantzakis recognizes in his famous work *Zorba the Greek*: "The highest point a (person) can attain is not knowledge, or virtue, or goodness, or victory, but something even greater, more heroic, more despairing: sacred awe."[8]

Awe flows from clarity in the way we see and experience life. During a visit to Japan I was invited to visit the most holy Shinto temple in Japan, Ise Jingu. During the visit a director of the shrine who used to be a forester there took me onto one of the bridges and, through the Catholic religious sister who acted as our interpreter, asked me to look at the water and tell him what struck me about it. I told him that it seemed to be crystal clear.

To this statement he nodded, smiled, and said: "Now listen, what do you hear?" I said: "It sounds like a frog."

"Yes," he responded. "It is a frog, but a very special frog. It is a species that only lives near clear water. You will not find it anywhere else on the grounds near water that is stagnant or not as clear as this brook."

The same can be said of our sense of the presence of God in our lives. When we are so preoccupied with worry that we have no time to quiet our souls and to help our hearts be still, we run the risk of missing God in certain wonderful ways. When we pray, how often do we say: "Speak, Lord, for your servant is listening"? More often, I think, we say: "Listen, Lord, for your servant is speaking!"

Life in general, sad to say, is often like this as well. We are preoccupied with control, worry, and the need to see "purpose" in the things around us, and so we have no sense of balance in our lives. Our lives are not fed by a fresh spring of reality. Rather, we live a stagnant existence tethered to our needs, fears, and desires—much of which are fed by often well-meaning people around us.

How often do our family and friends unconsciously decide that the "music" of anxiety and worry needs to be played in life? When there is peace they are nervous. I have an acquaintance who always calls and inquires after my health in a way that makes it sound that I am sick but hiding it from him. How many of us have people in our lives like this? This type of person tends to see the sad side of life or make us into someone who is too busy, under too much stress, or certainly suffering in some way.

This is not done consciously or with any malice in mind. We are all trained for it and when we try to break such patterns, it throws off the other person involved. But such an attitude stifles our ability to see life clearly, to appreciate it with wonder and awe.

Once I was traveling to Ireland to give a week-long workshop. The person meeting me at the plane said: "Oh, you poor sock you!" When I responded with puzzlement at the comment, the person said: "Oh, you must be terribly tired after the trip."

"Actually, I feel pretty good, even with the time change. I took a week off before this long trip and the plane ride was a lot of fun."

"But," she pressed on, "you'll be teaching here for a week and I'm sure that will be quite a bit for you." "Well," I responded, "I can understand your concern but I love this country. And even though it is very beautiful, even more beautiful than the surrounding countryside are the people themselves."

"Oh, but after the week, you will be back at work again won't you?" she persisted.

"Well, actually I shall be off for a week first and then I'll be teaching at St. Michael's College in Vermont, which I also love. I don't know why they even pay me!"

"Oh, more teaching again. My, that must be quite a bit after being here."

Undaunted, I added with the hopes of helping her realize I wasn't a burnout case: "Oh, but then I plan to take another week off at Martha's Vineyard."

Finally she paused, looked at me in a funny way and said: "My, but you take a lot of time off!"

It is very easy to fall into the rhythm of a life of business, worry, complaints, hurrying, ignoring, and resentment. The tempo of the sensitive life is something different. It is one in which we pay attention; we are alert to what is happening and really take note of the people and life around us. Sensitive people slow down the frames of life because they value the process rather than the products of interactions. If only more of us were like that.

In Thailand, as I rushed around through many of the areas which had artisans and traders, they would continually try to slow me down by showing me how the lacquerware or silver jewelry was fashioned. The point was that they believed I would value them and their work more if I became a part of the step by step process which led up to the valued end.

Awe is based on a valuing process—even when we don't know what the end product will be. Awe seeks to open everything that imprisons the clarity of meaning. We can easily see the beauty in a blooming rose or a tulip. But in other cases, such as the human person, the magnificence is hidden. Only patience, attention, and ultimately deep sensitivity will unleash awe-inspiring reality.

As is possible with anything good, awe can be defeated very easily. Each one of us does it in so many ways and we don't even realize it. People can be heard saying: "Oh, if only I had an opportunity to visit a new land or meet someone special or do something really exciting." Others read books on mysticism, spirituality, and prayer, and say: "I wish I were like that Zen *roshi*, Taoist sage, Hindu guru, Jewish rabbi, Christian saint, or Russian *staretz*; he or she experiences so much that seems so deep and wonderful in life."

What we don't often realize (unless we are quite mindful in this area) is that the opposite is true. For most of us, it is not that we don't have the opportunities; it is that we fail to avail ourselves of the opportunities that are there now because of obstacles to daily mysticism that we have failed to uncover or remove. The good news about each of these blocks to sensitivity and awe is that they usually dissolve when we gain a simple sense of perspective. And it is to this topic that we will now turn.

5. *A Simple Sense of Perspective*

Encountering simplicity in life is wonderful for with it comes a true sense of what's important. When we are simple people we are sensitive to ourselves and life in a way that we tend to see things in their proper perspective. In turn, with perspective our life—even during pain and confusion—has a sense of simplicity and direction which never totally disappears, although it may be partially hidden from us at the time. It is something delicate yet strong which doesn't depend on our emotional state or the impact of others.

Yet, having perspective can be an elusive undertaking no matter how aware we try to be. Even when we think we have it and are being sensitive, we may not. This is illustrated well in the following story told by Stephen Covey:

> One Sunday morning (I was) on a subway in New York. People were sitting quietly—some reading newspapers, some lost in thought, some resting with their eyes closed. It was a calm, peaceful scene.
>
> Then suddenly, a man and his children entered the subway car. The children were so loud and rambunctious that instantly the whole climate changed.
>
> The man sat down next to me and closed his eyes, apparently oblivious to the situation. The children were yelling back and forth, throwing

things, even grabbing people's papers. It was very disturbing. And yet, the man sitting next to me did nothing.

It was difficult not to feel irritated. I could not believe that he could be so insensitive as to let his children run wild like that and do nothing about it, taking no responsibility at all. It was easy to see that everyone else on the subway felt irritated, too. So finally, with what I felt was unusual patience and restraint, I turned to him and said: "Sir, your children are really disturbing a lot of people. I wonder if you wouldn't control them a little more?"

The man lifted his gaze as if to come to a consciousness of the situation for the first time and said softly, "Oh, you're right. I guess I should do something about it. We just came from the hospital where their mother died about an hour ago. I don't know what to think, and I guess they don't know how to handle it either."

Can you imagine what I felt at that moment? My paradigm shifted. Suddenly I *saw* differently, I *thought* differently, I *behaved* differently. My irritation vanished. I didn't have to worry about controlling my attitude or my behavior; my heart was filled with the man's pain. Feelings of sympathy and compassion flowed freely. "Your wife just died? Oh, I'm so sorry! Can you tell me about it? What can I do to help?" Everything changed in an instant.[9]

Perspective relies on a number of attributes. Chief among them is taking oneself lightly. Michel de Montaigne said: "No one is exempt from talking nonsense. The misfortune is to do it solemnly." It is very easy to take oneself too seriously because the world in which we live is indeed a serious place. If we take nothing to heart, then life is not very meaningful. On the other hand, if we swallow everything including our own image, then our life of meaning will not last very long. And so, humor can help us keep perspective, stay committed, and remain balanced.

Humor is essential to uncover in ourselves and others the hidden negatives that we harbor in our hearts and minds. For example, when I am annoyed or a bit depressed I often exaggerate things to draw out and demonstrate the nonsense that is sitting destructively within me. I also harass others in the same way when I feel that is what is going on with them. They eventually realize what I am doing, and we can laugh at the distorted, partially hidden beliefs that they, as well as I, so easily embrace.

Once a former classmate who is now a Catholic priest called me to ask if he might come over for dinner. As we sat relaxing before sitting down to eat, he mentioned that he was a little down because of his work the past six years as a vocation director. He told me about the difficulties of the work, how some members of his religious order couldn't understand the nature of his work wasn't just to get "new bodies" into the order, and that he was discouraged because of their attitude.

"Well, in six years how many new candidates for the priesthood have you gotten?" I asked.

Hearing this he made a face and responded: "You are so crass, Bob. 'How many have you gotten?' What a question to ask. The numbers aren't important. My work involves help-ing people discern their roles in life. If they wish to become priests, fine. If not, fine."

I pushed on: "Jim, how many have you gotten?"

He said a little exasperated now: "You just don't under-stand. Numbers aren't the issue, Bob. It's more than that."

I finally said: "Jim, stop equivocating; in the past six years how many have you gotten?"

To this he replied quietly: "None."

"None!" I said. "Well, no wonder you feel the way you do, you should be depressed. You are a *total* failure!"

Knowing me, he responded laughing: "Boy, am I glad I came to see you for help!"

After laughing together a bit over my outrageousness, he was able to speak in more detail about how, without realizing it, he had absorbed the sense of failure others felt about the lack of priestly vocations in the Catholic church. He could see that although he was saying the right things, he was believing something else without recognizing it. This was causing him more pain than he had realized.

Again and again we swallow so much that is negative and cover it over with claims to the contrary which sound so nice but mean little to our deep-down beliefs. So when we do feel bad about something, we ought to do our best not to suppress the feeling but to follow it. It will lead us to the erroneous thinking and beliefs that are quietly sitting in our minds and supporting it. Only by recognizing our distorted thinking can we then challenge the unnecessary negativity and rob it of its hidden power.

Humor also helps us to face the crazy expectations of others. Too often we allow ourselves to get pulled into situations where there are such great needs and we are slowly and imperceptibly drawn into trying to meet them without any sense of our own limits and needs. I think this is what Rev. Edward Jeffrey was thinking when he wrote in the June 14, 1964 issue of the *Observer* that "People expect the clergy to have the grace of a swan, the friendliness of a sparrow, the strength of an eagle, and the night hours of an owl—and some people expect such a bird to live on the food of a canary."

Finding Your Own Word

For many of us, living with our expectations of ourselves—as well as those of others—prevents us from really living sensitively. Too often the image we have of ourselves has been wrought early in life and we continue to move through our daily, weekly, monthly, and yearly activities as if on automatic pilot. Then we complain: "Where did the time go?" My oldest brother Ron once asked my father whether his sixty-eight years went by fast. My father looked at him, snapped his fingers, and said in a soft voice: "Just like that."

We can't prevent time from moving along. We can't avoid the natural presence of expectations—unreasonable and sensible. But we can have a better sense of identity. This makes living sensitively in the time we do have a greater possibility. Without it we are like observers, watching ourselves live, wandering in a "fog."

If we look at key classic and contemporary spiritual figures we can see how each was sensitive to his or her own personality style. They owned their identity and then lived life fully, with a real sense of self from God rather than the world. Mary's humility and courage, Peter's impetuosity, Francis of Assisi's passionate poverty, Ignatius of Loyola's obedience and analytic sense, Mother Teresa's simplicity, or Archbishop Desmond Tutu's honesty—all of them are spiritual lights to guide the rest of us in life. Contact with any of these persons and feeling the impact of their pure sense of self would cause changes in us. Just reading their words has an incredible effect on us.

But what of us? What do people discover when they come in contact with us? In most cases, they find a chameleon. We play so many roles that none of them is really true. The confusion that occurs on those occasions when we are in a room with people from many different parts of our lives (work, home, friends, school, the past, the present ...) only shows how fragmented we are.

We waste so much energy in being people we feel we should be, others want us to be, or we would like to be, rather than who we are being called to be by God. That is why it is essential to begin the search now for the identity we have been given by God. It of course is a lifelong journey, but one that is measured by involvement in the process rather than by achievement.

One approach to discovering our true identity is to find a word which we think describes who we truly are. For years I held onto the word "enthusiasm" as my word. It never seemed deep enough, but I lived and worked with it for I believed it described me best. After several years, the word "vitality" seemed to fit and had more substance to it. Then one day as I was walking along the Hudson River in New York State, I was overcome with a sense of sadness. I felt like a "little Moses," always pointing to the promised land for others but never getting there myself. At that point I realized my new word was "freedom." I felt that I was on the edge of freedom and this new word would hold me and encourage me to move to the next stage of my life. "Freedom" would be my new name.

Finding your word is sometimes a frustrating process though. There are many false starts since we put up so many fronts and don't let people near us to see what the heart of our soul and personality is. However, honest prayer, reflection, speaking with friends, and questioning the guides in one's life can help the journey toward finding one's true self and in turn, with this sensitivity to the truth about ourselves in hand, to appreciate the presence of God as well.

Accurate Self-Talk

Once we have a more correct word or name, we can then be freer and more integrated, we can be sensitive to all people in the same way. This will save energy and help us to develop as persons, instead of wasting the energy involved in trying to develop several personalities or faces simultaneously.

In addition, it will help us better monitor the messages we give ourselves all day. That is what is referred to in psychology as "self-talk." With a real sense of self we can approach situations with a greater sense of certainty and humility. Consequently, rather than seeking approval or reinforcement, we act out of our identity. If positive results occur fine; if negative ones occur, well, fine too.

When we can feel ourselves starting to be anxious, depressed, or under stress, we can ask questions that will get us back in touch with our true word and help us see that our fears or "dis-ease" are arising out of trying to play a role, fearing rejection, or being revealed for being a charlatan of some type. Some questions we need to ask ourselves when having negative feelings include:

1) Why am I making myself so angry in this situation?

2) What is it about this situation that is resulting in my making myself so uncomfortable?

3) What do I fear losing in this situation?

4) What am I demanding of the people around me and why is it so upsetting that I am not getting it?

5) What is the worst thing that could happen if I said or did _____?

6) Why am I so worried about the possibility of people seeing me as imperfect, unhelpful, a failure, not unique, uncaring, power hungry, greedy, addicted, or ignorant since in some instances it is certainly true?

7) What is the reason I am giving people the power to upset me?

8) What is the most helpful thing I can do in this instance to learn more about myself, the people I am dealing with, and God?

9) If I am alone, what is it that I am concentrating on in myself that is transforming solitude into loneliness and self-deprecation?

10) Why am I taking an annoying event and making it into something worse?

All the above questions, and ones like them which each person can make up, help us become more free. They are designed to break the spiritual logjam of expectations, fears, angers, anxieties, and stress. Then it becomes possible to live sensitively and fully rather than watch one's life pass by as an observer. They also produce a good deal of information on how we are not living out of our central identity (word), but instead are falling into patterns of pleasing, grasping, and controlling.

The freedom to live sensitively has a price though. It is honesty. And, the importance of honesty will be discussed in the opening chapter in the next section on sensitivity to others, as well as in the final one on sensitivity to God—a place where honesty is most important of all, for it is in this relationship that transformation truly becomes possible.

SENSITIVITY
TO OTHERS

THREE

Seeds of Sensitivity

Although sensitivity to others in its purest form seems so simple, it is still not an easy attitude to live out. Just as nonviolence can be falsely regarded as mere passivity, real sensitivity is sometimes mistakenly seen as weakness rather than real strength.

The reality is that we all think of ourselves as being sensitive but often this is far from the truth. Many times we think things are funny or insignificant, but that is often not how people receive our comments and actions. As the Greek proverb notes: "Though boys throw stones at frogs in sport, the frogs do not die in sport but in earnest." In seeking and appreciating the gift of sensitivity as something very precious, we must also accept the responsibility to search out and consider our existing deficiencies in this area and seek to correct them.

One of the best ways to do this is to "seed" our attitude with an increased awareness of these values:

- Silence and maintaining a sensitive listening stance,
- Risking involvement by foregoing the need for success and praise in every encounter,
- Appreciating the importance of perseverance, no matter what the apparent odds against us are,

- Assertively facing obstacles to sensitivity—including our own failures to see others as they are and could be,
- Appreciating our own foibles and "dark sides" with equanimity and necessary humor.

Silence and a Sensitive Listening Stance

To be sensitive to others and welcome a full expression of their uniqueness we need to provide silent spaces for people when they are with us. During such periods, they can think, breathe deeply, feel, and be invited to share themselves with us.

Silence which often provides a context for a sensitive listening stance is a valued commodity today because it is so rare. Sydney Smith once said about a friend: "He has occasional flashes of silence that make his conversation perfectly delightful." To this, I would add the following praise by Irish playwright, poet, and novelist Oscar Wilde for someone he knew who appreciated, as he did, the beauty of silence. Wilde said: "He knew the precise psychological moment to say nothing."

Silence is important not only for its concrete value, but also for its metaphorical worth. By this I mean that our culture is often so noisy with our (frequently white, male-centered) values that the unfortunate result is that sometimes both women and people of color somehow never get heard. When this occurs everyone loses.

This is partially what I think prompted Ann Clark to say: "How many women never 'find their voice' because in order to get to their art they would have to scream?"[1] Ruth Benedict, in her classic work *Patterns of Culture*, warns:

> There has never been a time when civilization stood more in need of individuals who are genuinely culture conscious, who can see objectively the social behavior of other people without fear and recrimination.[2]

A sensitive listening stance involves not only being open to the "voices" of people like ourselves, but also to persons of a different gender or color.

I recall two occasions when I keenly felt this issue of being both gender-sensitive and color-conscious. In the first instance I was teaching a course in Vermont. After the course I had individual meetings with the students to go over their work and to reflect with them on the course. One student who had done very well and seemed to be involved in the material commented that she had enjoyed the course immensely. However, she said that when I had shown a video at the end of the course in which a female poet spoke, she realized that the course was lacking in its presentation of the voices of women.

I readily agreed to this critique. But it wasn't until a few years later that I felt it more deeply myself. It was when Maya Angelou was scheduled to speak at a major religious education congress in Anaheim, California. As I sat there waiting for her to speak, an announcement was made that she was ill and would not be able to attend. The person who would be the speaker in her place was Yolanda King, the daughter of Martin Luther King, Jr. She turned out to be fantastic! The content of her talk was impressive, but even more than that the style and approach she took was what really exhilarated me.

The real surprise for me though came later. Even though I felt very fulfilled by her presentation, a few minutes after it was over I found something about it had deeply saddened me. I thought: "What could this be?" The presentation had been so wonderful. Then, as I walked away the reason came to me.

In my denomination, and in many other mainline churches and non-Christian faiths as well, the liturgies and homilies are stylized in such a very male, western European fashion. Because of this I and others have long been deprived of the richness of a multi-cultural approach of the female as well as male perspective on the spirituality of life. In most cases our life of worship has been too narrow to experience the richness of the living God.

In line with this, Audre Lorde also sums up our need to realize how we inadvertently see only part of the picture and miss the real value of listening, learning, and affectively experiencing life (from both a woman's and person-of-color's perspective). She says: "The White fathers told us: 'I think therefore I am,' and the Black mother within each of us—the poet—whispers in our dreams: I feel, therefore, I can be free."[3] How true this is. If we are to be sensitive we must truly be open to different ways of perceiving the world due to gender and culture. Otherwise, we are condemned to miss so much in our interactions with others and to dismiss the beautiful, different ways of understanding and communicating that people dissimilar to us manifest.

Risk and Freedom from the Need for Success and Praise

The existence of an honest sensitive attitude is sometimes best proven by the presence of a willingness to boldly risk and to fully commit oneself when it is necessary. Dietrich Bonhoeffer in his *Letters and Papers from Prison* wrote: "The essence of chastity is not the suppression of lust, but the total orientation of one's life toward a goal."[4]

This type of attitude is a rarity today in all phases of life—even in religion. As Jonathan Swift once said: "We have just enough religion to make us hate, but not enough to make us love one another."

An attitude of love and sensitivity sounds pretty, but in the concrete it takes a good deal of work and a willingness to risk. Yet willingness to risk is the most essential attitude that those of us wishing to experience a spiritually vibrant life must assume. Without a willingness to risk involvement in real relationships, loneliness, apathy, and an unhealthy preoccupation with self are all that remain. These can only lead to moodiness and eventually to despair.

Freedom from the need for results is important in this regard. Risk-taking is an attitude that starts anew each day. This is very much in line with a constant willingness to venture out, even when we really can't see secure results. The outcome of such an attitude is one in which life replaces existence. Interaction replaces inaction.

No matter how hot it may be walking along the Tiber in Rome, or how wet one becomes while rushing through the rain on the Strand in London, such actual experiences are much more exhilarating than sitting in one's cool, dry living room reading a fancy travel guide. People afraid to risk use up all their energy dreaming about doing great things or taking important chances and then have little energy or courage left to take the first step. People of real vision expend some energy dreaming (looking at life's "travel guide"), but have more than enough left to act.

If we know this, what keeps us from risking? Many things to be sure, but certainly anxiety is frequently reported to be a key factor. But as crazy as it may sound on first blush, the question can be asked of people of faith: What is the real use of being anxious? Jesus himself asked: "How can you change things one iota by worrying?" And, as the French saying goes: "One meets his destiny often on the road he takes to avoid it." Whether we do this by avoiding, "over-thinking," or procrastinating (while all the time fooling ourselves into believing we are planning and discerning), the results (or lack of them!) will show us the bad fruits of our hesitancy.

Sometimes, instead of going off and pondering something we need a Twelve-Step approach which says: Don't think your way into a new way of action, but act your way into a new way of living. In such cases we need to rely more on the right side of the brain, on our intuition, to balance our left-brain style which relies on cognition alone. Otherwise, we may never leave our secure place in the status quo at all.

John Philip Sousa once said "Jazz will endure just as long as people hear it through their feet instead of their brains." The same can be said metaphorically of living the sensitive life. Living it requires more than discernment, more than just thinking things through. It also requires acting upon our intuitions and caring feelings.

This does not mean that reflection isn't valuable or risking is the same as being rash. Being rash is the result of thoughtless impulse. Risking is knowing there are some things we must do—even when we feel they may involve making mistakes or even failure. The reality we must be willing to look at and accept is: being on the road to finding the truth or seeking improvement is, at best, a hazardous process. Still, it is one we cannot avoid if we wish to live a full spiritual life, even when the temptation to hold back seems so sensible.

Once there was a young, would-be writer who was finishing his final project. When the instructor who had been reviewing the final draft of his work met with him, he suggested to the young man that the story was indeed good, but to be truly great the plot needed further development. As he walked away, the young man thought to himself: "This is good now; in terms of a grade it probably is a B. If I try to improve it by tinkering with the plot, I might mess up what I have already done."

The risk was to improve or stay put, and this is the same challenge we all face, whether at small or significant turning points in our life. Unfortunately, when faced with this challenge, because of our fear of failure and criticism, we too often hold back. We spend so much time worrying about what people will think, or whether we will miss the mark. Instead, we need to put such undue concerns in their proper place so we are not blackmailed by the critics in our environment.

In *The Te of Piglet* Benjamin Hoff helps us put this problem in perspective through the following story:

> While traveling separately through the countryside late one afternoon, a Hindu, a Rabbi, and a Critic were caught in the same area by a terrific

thunderstorm. They sought shelter at a nearby farmhouse.

"That storm will be raging for hours," the farmer told them. "You'd better stay here for the night. The problem is, there's only room enough for two of you. One of you'll have to sleep in the barn."

"I'll be the one," said the Hindu. "A little hardship is nothing to me." He went out to the barn.

A few minutes later there was a knock on the door. It was the Hindu. "I'm sorry," he told the others, "but there is a cow in the barn. According to my religion, cows are sacred, and one must not intrude into their space."

"Don't worry," said the Rabbi. "Make yourself comfortable here. I'll go to sleep in the barn." He went out to the barn.

A few minutes later, there was a knock at the door. It was the Rabbi. "I hate to be a bother," he said, "but there is a pig in the barn. I wouldn't feel comfortable sharing my sleeping quarters with a pig."

"Oh, all right," said the Critic. "I'll go sleep in the barn." He went out to the barn.

A few minutes later, there was a knock at the door. It was the cow and pig.[5]

The lesson: we can't let our fear of critics hold us back from risking sensitivity to others. Spiritual success is sometimes best measured not by what we accomplish, but by whether we have the tenacity to persevere when we don't see immediate results.

Perseverance

Perseverance is a virtue which we do not always sufficiently value. We need to recognize the value of an attitude which encourages us not to turn back, even when temporary failure occurs. Perseverance has long been considered a trait of great spiritual value, for as it states in the Koran: "God blesses those who persevere."

Perseverance enables us to move from a sensitive awareness of situations—even those involving injustice—into a willingness to act, even in the most difficult circumstances. I saw this recently in many of the people of Cambodia, a country which has the largest percentage of handicapped persons in the world. This is due to the violent period under Pol Pot and the Khmer Rouge known as "the killing fields." It is also because of injuries caused by the continued presence of land mines. They still cover one third of the country and it is estimated that it will take one hundred years to clear them completely from the land. And even this figure is not considered accurate since plastic land mines float during floods in the rainy season and move from uncleared areas into previously-considered safe zones.

Several years ago, a number of the government pensioners in Cambodia who were handicapped had their disability payments interminably delayed. Despite their constant complaints nothing was done, and they knew that any effort to stage a major protest in the capital city of Phnom Penh might be blocked by the army.

As a result, these individuals got up about midnight and joined together to march on the capital. They knew that by starting in the middle of the night, they would be able to get too close to the center of the city by dawn to be stopped by the surprised army. Yet, to do this the paraplegics and other disabled persons needed to cooperate. And so, the persons in the wheelchairs (who had their legs blown off by land mines) had to be the eyes for the blind pensioners who pushed them along in makeshift wheelchairs on the dusty roads leading into the capital.

When you think of this protest being mounted in the dark by these people, you wonder how they could do it. Yet by working in community they did. They risked. They persevered. And, they embarrassed the government enough to get their pensions resumed. Amazing!

Too often sensitivity ceases when we focus too much on the odds we are up against instead of being more aware of the holiness of being involved with other persons and causes—no matter what the outcome!—that we are concretely faced with each day. When we see the work of Mother Teresa of Calcutta we are not just left with the overwhelming problem she and her sisters have to face each day, instead we are more surprised by their continued sensitivity to the plight of the dying people they meet and embrace. Perseverance is encouraged then when we don't lose sight of the importance of doing what we can rather than being lost in how terrible the overall situation is at any point in time.

Generosity

Generosity must also be at the core of an attitude of sensitivity. In true generous behavior there is a profound recognition of the reality emphasized by the Yiddish proverb: "Shrouds are made without pockets." In other words, so often we worry about ourselves and our own sense of security that we actually forget that the best way to be a self-confident and faithful friend of God is to be more sensitive to the needs of others, rather than becoming overly concerned with ourselves. And so, we need an appreciation of both the wonder of giving, the death-like quality of greed, and the neurotic concern many of us have (certainly including me) with being taken advantage of by those to whom we give something. Otherwise, we will be trapped in the moody, emotional prison of over-preoccupation with self.

In reality, much of our giving is conditional and is really not very wonderful after all. But when we are truly sensitive and do give freely and spontaneously we set the stage for simple acts of wonder, as is shown in the following reflection by a young seminarian working in Central America:

> Once, at a beach outing, one of the girls who couldn't swim was tossed about in the rocks in a lagoon. I did not hesitate to try to rescue her amidst the laughing of the guys because I too was tossed about like a rag doll. Despite the difficulties involved, I somehow persevered and we both managed to get

out alive, although I did wind up suffering badly with cuts and bruises.

The real surprise for me though was that only later did it occur to me that I myself couldn't swim! And although I spoke little of the incident to others, this whole episode and the implications of it intrigued me. My sense was I found that the bottom line of the whole encounter was life and its importance.

I think there is something within all of us that makes potential heroes, and that a hero's journey can be a mystical experience. As the theologians Karl Rahner and Meister Eckhart believed, mystical experiences happen everyday. I believe that by learning to let go of ourselves, we are placed on the hero's journey of self-discovery, and ultimately the discovery of God within us.[6]

The generosity involved in his sensitivity and action in behalf of the drowning girl set the stage for him to discover more about himself and his God. Generosity, when it is at the source of our attention to others, produces good results for all involved—even though we may not clearly see them at the time.

Friendship as a Path to Sensitivity

The strength of sensitivity also lies in our being able to embrace qualities of friendship which allow us to learn as well as to give, to share as well as to guide, to be unique as well as to have things in common, and to seek all that can be sought rather than to hold each other back in fear. Theologian Sallie McFague, in her book *Models of God* speaks of such a type of friendship when she points to five qualities of friendship in her chapter "God as Friend."[7] They are also of value to us here when looking at relationships.

1) Friendship is based on *parity*. A friend who neither rescues nor victimizes is someone to be valued. Interdependency is a value that gives in different ways, at different times, to both friends.

2) Friendship is *open*, which means friends are free to come and go. How unfortunate it is that some people only know relationships which are imprisoning rather than freeing. We see this especially in the case of women and children involved with people who abuse them.

3) There is an *inclusive* element in friendship which does not limit the relationship to only two persons. Instead, there is a freedom which encourages the enrichment of each other; it is based on personal self-esteem and a genuine wish for the development of the other person.

4) Friendship allows, even rewards *diversity*. Unlike the patriarchal experiences, friends do not request compliance but encourage a diversity and new collaboration which helps them to see things in new ways too.

5) Friendship implies *growth* because friends, real friends, welcome change rather than worship the status quo.

The values of parity, openness, inclusivity, diversity, and growth are all found in the following Middle Eastern story from *A Thousand and One Nights*. It is a loosely based version of "The Tale of the Sixth Barber's Brother:"

> The great palace of the family Barmachi in Baghdad was a place of great food, joy, and revelry. One day, a beggar stopped by this house and entered and asked the master of the house if he might have food and shelter.

> The master greeted him with warmth and the invitation: "Ah, there is nothing for it but that you stay here and share my meal with me, eating the salt of my cloth." "I thank you master," said the beggar, "for I can fast no longer."

> And then his host called out, "Come, you others and spread out the cloth quickly and let us eat for this poor man is hungry." And so numerous servants hurried in and made a great show of running to and fro as if they were spreading a cloth and covering it with many meats and groaning dishes. But all they did was gesture with bare and empty hands.

And so, when the master said, "Seat yourself at my side, dear guest, and hasten to do honor to my entertainment," the beggar sat down beside him at the edge of the imaginary cloth. And the old man moved his hands about as if he were touching the dishes and taking samples from them, and he moved his lips and jaws as if chewing, and he said to the beggar, "What do you have to say about these dishes on your left? Those heavenly roast chickens, stuffed with pistachios, almonds, rice, raisins, peppers, cinnamon, and the paste of lamb! The aroma, my friend, the aroma!"

"Allah be good to us," cried the beggar. "Never was there such an aroma. These birds are the soul of all birds and their stuffing, a poem." "You display a well-bred indulgence to my kitchen, my friend," said the old man. "Ah, now if I may, I'll give you a mouthful of this other dish with my own fingers. And the beggar reached forward with his lips, opened his mouth and took a great swallow. And then with closed eyes, he said, "As Allah lives, it is perfection, and I say without fear of contradiction, that never elsewhere have I tasted such eggplants. In the stuffing, I detect the hand of an artist, the shredded lamb, the chickpeas, the pine nuts, the cardamon, the nutmeg, the cloves, the ginger, the pepper, the aromatic herbs. I taste them as a whole and I taste them separately, so exquisite is the blending."

After this, the old man then said, "Remove the cloth and bring on dessert." And when it came he proceeded in the same way as during the main courses until the beggar suddenly jumped up, lifted his arm so high, and brought it down so violently on the old man's neck that the whole hall echoed with the slap. And raising his arm again, he struck more violently than before.

And at this, the old man grew very angry and cried, "What are you doing, O vilest of earth's creatures?" And the beggar replied, "Master and crown of my head, I am your obedient slave whom you have weighed to the dust with gifts. Whom you have received in your house, whom you've nourished at your cloth with the choicest meats such as kings have never tasted; whose soul you have sweetened with your conserves, your compotes, and your finest pastries. What would you, my lord? I have taken so much of your finest hospitality that I am mad, and I've raised my hand against my savior. Pity your slave then and since your soul is higher than my soul forgive the madness wrought in me by your wonderful generosity."

And at this response, the old man laughed heartily, had the real feast brought in, and the two of them became fast friends. And the Scheherazade concludes the story that they ate and drank and lived in sweet luxury for the next twenty years. A happy ending to a frustrating story.[8]

When we think about the existence of sensitivity to others, one has to think that what non-whites and females are sometimes experiencing is akin to the Barmecide Feast in the preceding story. Everyone speaks about equality and says that all are made in the image and likeness of God (*imago dei*), but the realities don't support this claim in many cases.

Many women and people of color say that they are told they are equal and that people are sensitive to their needs, teachings, and heritage, but really aren't. If we wish to claim the mantle of sensitivity then, the question that confronts us is: how do we live with a hope of beginning the real feast of equality with an embrace of the joy of diversity when the reality seems so far off?

Well, maybe it can start with us, with our vision, with our actions, with our real belief in the value of the strength of sensitivity over the weakness of cultural and gender-based ignorance. If this is truly our goal, so much more will be gained by all. But this will take risk and perseverance. And, are we really ready to commit ourselves to this?

The Obstacle of Prejudice

Respect and sensitivity for others go hand in hand. Prejudice is not reasoned into people as adults, so it cannot be reasoned out. Instead it is something we learn pre-verbally and nonverbally from many sources before we have the cognitive skills to consider what we are being taught.

Unfortunately, often our prejudices are hidden under what we consider to be perfectly reasonable "oughts." As Thomas Merton, the Catholic contemplative noted:

> It is both dangerous and easy to hate man as he is because he is not "what he ought to be." If we do not first respect what he is we will never suffer him to become what he ought to be: in our impatience we will do away with him altogether.[9]

Massive projection may be disguised as supposed sensitivity on our part as well, so we need to be alert to this possibility too. A good example of this is the reactions of many people to the atrocities in Bosnia during the breakup of Yugoslavia. To feel the horror about the rape of Muslim women is correct; to want to take every possible action to prevent this from continuing to happen again is, to my mind, even more correct! (As you can surmise, I'm not much of a passivist on this issue.) However, to hate *all* Serbs in the world because of this and in the process to avoid the unconscious reality of our own inhuman tendencies is wrong. Instead, we need to more often mimic Abraham Lincoln's philosophy of relationship which is best typified by his statement: "I don't like that man. I have to get to know him better."

Furthermore, we need to recognize that all people are very different—especially when they are in emotional or physical pain. We can even see this very clearly with respect to animals. For example, when a cat is sick, it walks away, hides, and wants to be left alone. On the other hand, what do dogs do when they are sick? They're dramatic actors who lie underfoot in the middle of the kitchen floor moaning and drooling as if to say: "Do something! Can't you see I'm sick?"[10] Similar differences can also be seen with people and this fact must be recognized to achieve results whether they be physical, psychological, or spiritual in nature.

If a physician treated everyone who came to her consultation room door as if he needed a splenectomy, she would certainly have uneven surgical results. If a psychologist didn't have a broad enough theory of personality to allow for individual differences, he would erroneously and simplistically treat everyone exactly as if the person were like himself. In the few cases where this was so there might be some measure of success, but in most instances since there are natural personality differences, failure would no doubt result.

So, just as in counseling or medicine all people are not considered to be alike, so must the case be in life in general, as well as in our sensitivity to the spiritual wonders and talents of each person we meet. We must begin to appreciate others for their wonderful but sometimes hidden uniqueness. As the Yiddish proverb goes: "If all pulled in one direction, the world would keel over." Once we recognize this, our views of and interactions with others can become more rich and less filled with stress, disappointment, and a sense of being judgmental. Instead we are called and challenged to recognize and reflect the spiritual gifts of others so they can own and build on them, rather than let them lay fallow or atrophy.

This lesson was particularly of use with one group of Franciscan friars who were having a distressing time. Each year they took out time for peer evaluations, evaluating each other and providing feedback. Often this was a very negative process, and they wanted to recast it so it would be a more fruitful and positive experience while retaining its honesty.

In response, I simply suggested that in doing their peer evaluations they make an effort first to determine what

different gifts were displayed in each person being considered and to describe them in as great detail as possible.
Then after this, when reflecting on the "sins" of their fellow
friars they could look for those times and instances when the
persons they were evaluating became anxious, upset, angry,
passive, or depressed and thus "psychologically" tripped
over their wonderful unique traits by either exaggerating,
minimizing or using them in an abusive fashion. The result:
a process of being sensitive to others that didn't forsake the
truth and at the same time didn't overlook or minimize the
unique beauty of each person.

Dealing with Failure

Once when I presented a lecture on involvement, spontaneity, and being a gentle presence in the world, one person
said to me: "You make being a sensitive person sound so
positive. But I have this fearful question nagging me. What
if I fail?"

I responded: "Well, let me assure you then. You will
fail!"

At this, the student's eyes opened wide, she made a face
and said: "Oh, great! Thanks!" and then the whole class
including the two of us laughed.

The reality though is that to attempt to live a sensitive
life brings with it a certain amount of failure and the part of
this failure which hurts the most is the recognition of the
personal limits, poor motivations, and personal inadequacies we have hidden from ourselves. The problem with
intimacy with people in pain is that while we try to help them
trust and open themselves to their inadequacies and faults,
we are called to see the blemishes which sit alongside the gifts
we have as well.

In my case, for example, I always thought of myself as
a generous person who had a hard time setting limits for
people. But over the years I have come to see more and more
that instead of being true to myself and others, the reality is
at times that I am a fake. One reason for this is I like to look

good and promise others more than I can deliver. Then when people call on me to deliver, I pull back and think to myself that they are asking too much.

If I were willing to know myself better, I could provide a more realistic welcome to others, prevent hurt on their part, and also head off the sadness I feel when people are angry or upset with me because I have let them down. And so, the questions I must face continually are: Am I willing to give up being a showman in the friendship I offer people but sometimes don't really mean? Am I also willing to recognize the hurt that bravado and false generosity (sometimes alcohol-induced) can produce?

As you can imagine, it's not so easy for me to have such truthful eyes. I guess it isn't for anyone who wants to be an honest, vulnerable healer in concrete situations rather than a person of love in the abstract sense. Abstract love never involves risk or failure, just good wishes and a rich imagination. Still, love in the concrete often is not pretty but its results are wonderful if we are willing to take the chance to encounter ourselves honestly as we open ourselves to others in ways in which we are willing to follow through on our promises and commitment.

Concrete love also calls us as persons seeking to be sensitive to ask the right question in relationships. How often we ask: "Would you like to have what I want to give you?" When the real question of love is: "What is it that you want and need?"

The second question is much more difficult because the answer is unpredictable. To fulfill the request we may even have to be (God forbid!) inconvenienced or taken out of our way and made temporarily uncomfortable. We may also have to admit the limits of our ability to fill the need being requested, because of our own situation or personality and admit this inadequacy on our part. Maybe this is why being a real healing presence in action, even though it sounds truly very noble and beautiful, is sometimes also very difficult to offer others.

From what I have noted thus far then, it is obvious that the conversion of others further transforms us in the process as well. It puts us and our promises on the line. I guess that is why when the combination of sensitive compassion and integrity in reaching out to others is present, the results are amazing and powerful for all involved ... including us!

Appreciating Ourselves and Recognizing Our Foibles

A final way to strengthen our ability to be sensitive to others is to readily appreciate ourselves and recognize our own foibles to the point where we can gently laugh at ourselves. When people enjoy themselves and can get in touch with their own beauty, they can even reach the point of teasing themselves. This is a wonderful illustration of the sensitivity people can have about themselves which then frees them to be more open to others instead of being overly protective due to unnecessary problems with public self-image or self-esteem. As a result, when this happens we can enjoy their own recognition of the foibles they have through the sense of humor they display about them. In my travels I have seen this with many groups, but particularly enjoy it with the wonderful people of Newfoundland and Ireland.

I have been to Newfoundland many times. But the first time I was there doing some consultant work, I particularly remember the flight back to Baltimore. I had just seated myself when a fellow dropped into the seat next to me, leaned over, and said to me: "Are you from Newfoundland? Are you a Newfee?" After I responded in the negative, he quickly followed with the question: "Well then, do you know where the Newfees keep their armies?" "No, I said." To this he replied: "Up their sleevies!" Making a face and laughing I said: "We're not going to do this for the whole flight are we?"

Then just after that, a really chipper old fellow from one of the French areas of Newfoundland who was sitting three rows in front of us, pulled down his fiddle from the overhead rack and started to sing and play. What a flight it was! What wonderful people Newfoundlanders are. I love them. Their joy and ability to poke fun at their own sense of simplicity made me more easily relax, accept my own ordinariness more, and better feel the sense of joy that was deep within me.

A similar thing happened to me when in Ireland. The Irish are a beautiful people who know the richness they demonstrate as poets, artists, writers, singers, and people of deep faith and hospitality. However, in knowing their gifts, they are also aware of some of the darkness they carry around in themselves and freely tease about it in jokes and quips.

One Irish fellow told me he had a wonderful trip to Miami and upon his return he expected the weather to be bitter and cold. Instead, he found it to be just delightful. Beside himself with the joy of this, he commented to an older woman who was seated in the spot beside him on the bus from the airport: "My, but what a beautiful day it is." To which she replied: "Ah yes, and you can bet we'll be paying for it down the road!"

It's wonderful when we can laugh at ourselves, our dark side, and our foibles. Without such an ability to do so, there is a tendency to bury our negative style through denial or bravado. When we do, we decrease our own sensitivity to self (self-awareness) and, in turn, increase our defensiveness with others.

Sensitivity and a sense of humor go well together. They set the stage for us to relax enough to see ourselves honestly, not take ourselves too seriously, and to learn how we can best be a sensitive healing presence to others without unduly carrying the burden of our pride. The joy of being at ease with oneself is a great and gentle gift; without it, sensitivity to others becomes just another chore rather than a wonder to experience even in the darkest of times.

FOUR

A Sensitive
Healing Presence

In addition to the general values of silence, risk, perseverance, the need to put failure in perspective, and seeing from a slightly different vantage point how important generosity and friendship are, there are some other very beautiful basics which will help us in offering a sensitive presence to others that are worth remembering as well. They have been recommended and used successfully by clinicians and spiritual guides down through the years. They are simple helps to enable all of us to be a more effective presence to others by providing a logic which can be applied in most situations, even when we walk in darkness.

Without such a structure in mind, otherwise avoidable mistakes in healing interactions are almost inevitable. Some of the more common mistakes are:

- The offering of premature advice,
- Feeling uncomfortable and unnecessarily helpless when speaking with persons who are sharing their pain,
- Intimating that persons should and can "get over it" by forgetting their abuse or loss,
- Running away from those in pain while seeming to offer help. (I see this last phenomenon particularly

present in persons confronted by grieving individuals or adult survivors of childhood sexual abuse. They do things like suggest reading a helpful book. But they do it in a way in which they are really saying: "Your grief and pain is making me feel uncomfortable and helpless. Go read this book, get better, then come back.")

It is helpful to learn or recall a few basic points about being sensitive and reaching out to others in need in an effort to enhance one's natural helping and relational skills. Whether preparing for therapy or a spiritual guidance session, supervising counselors, or speaking to a group of caring adults on how to be a better friend to others, I find emphasizing certain main elements of the helping process to be useful for all caring adults. No matter how sophisticated or elemental one's talents or skills are, awareness or a review of such a structure, can be of immeasurable assistance in being a sensitive healing presence—especially when there is emotion in the air and one feels overwhelmed by what one is being told or asked.

The suggested simple structure I am referring to which has proved fairly successful in most instances includes:

- Allowing people to tell their story,
- Simple summarization skills,
- Encouraging self-care.

Briefly looking at each of these elements here will help reveal their simple but real value.

Allow People to Tell Their Story

To say that you should allow family, friends, and acquaintances approaching you in need to tell their story may seem self-evident, but if we think about it for a minute I believe we can recognize that it really isn't. For instance, how often have you tried to tell people how you feel or what has happened to you when you were upset or excited only to have them repeatedly interrupt to give advice or tell you how a similar thing happened to them?

How often we don't get a chance to tell our story and this is a shame because having the ability to share our life with others is important. Telling one's story is especially beneficial in today's insensitive and ofttimes "psychologically-deaf" society because it:

- Allows one to present and release positive and negative emotions,
- Provides needed information,
- Gives the person an opportunity to relax and regress,
- Offers a needed opportunity for the person to reenact the story,
- Gives the person the feeling they have been truly heard.

In addition, when others have been given the space to share their ideas, hopes, frustrations, fears, angers, and anxieties in a safe environment, they are apt to see new possibilities on their own. But maybe, of even greater import, when people have shared intense emotions and they find the other person doesn't quickly try to cure the problem, minimize it, or become overwhelmed by it to the point of pulling back in the process, it is reassuring, refreshing, and healing in and of itself.

Encouraging another to tell his or her story is best communicated when one sits down and gives the nonverbal message: "I'm ready to listen." It is also fostered by asking for illustrations and starting the conversation with a general question such as: "Well, I can see you are upset. What exactly happened?" In this way the person can take the cue from you that you wish to listen sensitively so they can spend the time by sharing in vivid terms what they wish to tell you.

Simple Summarization Skills

In hearing someone's story, a plethora of information comes across. However, there are certain elements that should be looked for so they can be reflected upon and summarized. These include:

- Their chief complaint,
- Other possibly related issues or problems,
- What they did in the situation and how effective or satisfying their efforts were,
- What their needs, desires, demands, joys, and frustrations were in this particular setting,
- The parts other figures played in the story.

When this information is gathered and summarized, a better understanding and sense of what to do next can emerge. (This may simply be the recognition that one needs to have patience as in the case of newly-experienced grief.)

Provide Permission to Nourish Self

Although there are many different problems which require differential treatment too extensive to be discussed here, in today's world there are a great many people who are experiencing or have experienced great loss, abuse, or hurt. In such cases, there is a real need to give such persons encouragement to:

- Take care of themselves better physically, emotionally, and spiritually,
- To take any steps they can to have more accurate self-esteem (reflect on positive feedback from friends, list and value what they can do well, develop a careful inventory of the ways they have been kind and helpful to people through the years ...),
- Build balance in their lives by ensuring the key pieces of life and time to appreciate them are in place (i.e., prayer, work, relaxation, shopping, reading, visiting/calling friends, etc.).

When they do this on an ongoing basis, self-care can begin to replace self-condemnation and harmful types of self-denial.

Listening, summarizing, and nourishing then are three of the simplest, yet most important gifts we can give people in our desire to be sensitive to them and their needs. When we remember and apply them it is possible for some direction and clarity in the situation to emerge. It may not be toward an immediate solution, for there may not be one. But it will set the stage for a collaborative effort to look for small steps to take and the beginnings of discernment with respect to long-term decisions, and this in itself can be an important part of the healing process for people.

Walking with Others in Darkness

The simple general principles touched upon up to this point have one overriding theme: namely, knowing how to be sensitive and reach out to others not only involves standing with others in their pain to see in what direction they wish to go, but also that in the process we must find God in a gentle place within us in order to come to terms with our own fears, pain, doubts, and anxieties. To do this we must have some appreciation for a sense of our own darkness.

"Darkness" is a spiritual theme which is as central to sacred scripture as it is to contemporary life. Although the search for the "Light" of peace, love, joy, faith, and hope are worthy goals of discernment and daily theological reflection, darkness is always a presence not to be taken lightly or avoided. Otherwise, blindness and an existence centered on running from being sensitive to the necessary crosses in life will result.

In the well known passage from Luke 24:13-35, the Road to Emmaus, such blindness (a form of darkness) was a theme that was carefully addressed and emphasized. To recall it for a moment, two disciples of Jesus were walking along the road after his crucifixion. They met the resurrected Jesus but did not know him. During the journey when he inquired about their downcast mood, the irony of their blindness came through as they:

- Expressed surprise that Jesus did not seem to know about the recent occurrences in Jerusalem and they went on to admonish him for his ignorance,

- Shared their heartbreak, disillusionment, and dashed hopes,
- Demonstrated that their faith was shaken because they insisted on clinging to an image of God that was their own.

In verse 31 they began to move from doubt and a lack of recognition to recognition and faith. They did this when they began to see that scripture had called for the necessity of suffering, death, and resurrection. Then in verse 32 they began to experience Jesus as their hearts were burning and this had an important impact as well. But it was in the meal, in the breaking of the bread, the hospitality, that their darkness was dispelled. The presence of the resurrected Jesus broke through their previous notions of what the Messiah was to do and who he was to be (a Savior of power) to a new sensitivity to the Lord as a God who came into the world for one purpose: to love.

In the entire Lukan gospel, which may well be the most appropriate gospel for these dark times, the author wrote his lessons for a community who were probably third generation Gentiles far removed from Christianity's Judaic roots and the historical reality of Jesus. They hadn't walked the streets with him and weren't there to encounter the first days after the descent of the Holy Spirit on the apostles when everyone present could feel the love in the streets and personally experience the fervor of the early church.

Instead, they were a community much like us today. They had problems of faith and commitment as we do now. Just like us, they felt the darkness of the times and in trying to be sensitive to it in a meaningful way were drawn into temptations toward despair, greed, faithlessness, competition, narcissism, hopelessness, and withdrawal.

But in this passage, as in other places in this gospel, Luke used parallel themes and stories to connect for them and for us the historical Jesus with the resurrected Lord. Luke pointed out the ongoing presence of the Lord in this instance by pointing out the transition from the feeding of

the multitude to the last supper to the breaking of the bread
in the post-resurrection scene at Emmaus. Luke was challenging them in their ignorance (and us in our sense of
darkness) to move from a stoicism of heart to opening
themselves to the presence of a risen Jesus in their own
hearts, which is clearly still a valid challenge to us today.[1]

In being sensitive we need to be careful not to hold onto
the status quo or our vision of the way things should be. Just
as the persons walking on the road to Emmaus were called
to let go of their notion of what the Messiah should be like so
they could be sensitive to the presence of the real Jesus, we
are often called in a similar fashion to open our hearts to new
ways in which we can see the presence of God reflected in
others, ourselves, and our prayer life.

Facing Our Own Spiritual Darkness

Since the writing of Luke's gospel there have been many
other treatments of the theme of darkness. However, none is
perhaps as famous as the John of the Cross' "dark night of
the soul" which portrays spiritual darkness as a form of light
from God.

The suggestions he offers as to how one should behave
in prayer in such darkness are worth noting as a good
guideline for how we face the darkness today in both our
prayer life and daily way of living (our ethic). This advice is:

1) Be patient and trust that God has not aban-
doned you.

2) Rest in prayer and in God even though it
seems to be wasting time. Stay with the experience
and do not give up contemplative prayer.

3) Be free. Let go of the need to accomplish
something.

4) Be attentive. Keep on noticing God and what
God might be doing without forcing anything or
expecting the things to be the same as previously.

5) Be aware that for many the darkness comes
and goes.[2]

The positive point to note here is that there are benefits experienced by being in spiritual darkness when we don't run away from our dryness in prayer or our difficult interactions with others. Some of those advantages are:

- Increased motivation and determination to face the darkness in ourselves and others,
- Greater insight into one's personality style, defenses, values, gifts, spirituality, and areas of vulnerability,
- Less dependence on the recognition or approval of others,
- New skills and styles of behavior to complement our usual (possibly habitual) ways of interacting with others,
- Increased sensitivity to ourselves, God, and others,
- A sense of peace that is independent of external success, comfort, and security.

However, even with a recognition and acceptance of the value of these very real advantages, the perils and pressures for persons willing to be sensitive and present to others still remain.

A wonderful person with whom I had journeyed in therapy over a period of several years brought this point across to me when she said at a turning point in our time together: "I thought of the times I had reflected on the gifts of our relationship and how I liked to say, 'We both laughed, but I'm the only one who cries.' And it came to me that this was not quite true. That you also cry, but, mysteriously and sacrificially, you do so inwardly … maybe they are tears of the soul."

Jeffrey Kottler, author of the very fine work *On Being a Therapist* echoes a similar theme in a reflection on sensitive intimacy with persons in pain when he says:

Never mind that we catch their colds and flus, what about their pessimism, negativity, and psychopathology. You just cannot see somebody week after week, listen to their stories, and dry their tears without being profoundly affected by the experience. These are the risks for the therapist he will not recognize until years later. Images stay with us to the grave. Words creep back to haunt us. Those silent screams remain deafening.[3]

Consequently, we need to recognize such perils and note that in our intimacy with people in pain we are more vulnerable than we would be if we just didn't care.

The professionals in ministry, medicine, and psychology who come in to see me because of the pain in their own lives are often in my office by virtue of their vocation. If they weren't so sensitively involved in other people's lives they wouldn't have gotten their psychological and spiritual "fingers" so burned.

However, they also rightly realize that the answer is not to pull back, run away, and try to "medicate" themselves on such things as alcohol, work, or the search for power. What they seek is the peace of perspective so that they may still live and work humbly within the darkness without being overcome by it.

Although I go through a great deal with them in seeking a new attitude, form of thinking, and set of self-renewing behaviors so they can stay the course as helpers, one of the most important objectives is to help them realize that it is easy to fall into negative thinking when in a helping role. One of my goals then is to help them realize that their own silent "self-talk" will help them lose or keep perspective depending upon whether they are able to pick up their initial negative impressions and then address them sensibly.

The following is an example of this. While it is beneficial to caring physicians, nurses, priests, religious brothers and sisters, ministers, and psychotherapists, I believe it would be helpful for us all.

Self-Talk

1) *When you have made a mistake* remember to say to yourself: "Of course I have made a mistake. When you care you will make mistakes. The more you reach out, the more

mistakes you make. As a matter of fact if you are not making mistakes now and then, you are probably living too narrowly and diffidently because of an inordinate fear of what people will think if you fail."

2) *When people are angry at you* remember to say to yourself: "It is good that people feel they can be angry at me and don't have to worry that I will overreact in return. Just because they are angry at me doesn't make me a bad person or mean that their anger is capable of destroying me. It gives me a chance to practice poise in such situations and to assertively stand up for what I believe as a way to practice and model it for others."

3) *If you don't succeed* remember to say to yourself: "I can't reach everyone. I can try to be of help to different kinds of people, but it is dangerous for me to believe I am God or to accept the expectations some people put on me to have all the answers or to be able to meet all their demands in the way they want, and when they want."

4) *When you feel like a hypocrite* in suggesting steps to others on how to overcome resistances to growth and change that you don't take yourself remember to say to yourself: "Let me try to 'practice more often what I preach' so I can make this a more collaborative journey. I can practice more and more how to enter the 'promised land' of clarity, generosity, discipline, faithfulness, and love by following the tenets I propose."

5) *When you feel embarrassed* remember to say to yourself: "In a few weeks, months or years, what will all of this mean in terms of my life and salvation?"

6) *If you are about to have an outburst of anger* remember to say to yourself: "Why am I giving away the power? Let me hold back for a few minutes, hours, or days until I am clear enough to see if this is really important."

7) *When people don't listen*, don't appreciate what you do, or make fun of you remember to say to yourself: "Well, you can't win them all, can you?"

8) *When someone is indirectly hostile or passive-aggressive* (by procrastinating, etc.) remember to say to yourself: "Ah, he doesn't know he is behaving like this but all the same I have to be careful he doesn't get to me and in the process waste too much of my energy."

Final Comments

The walk in darkness with others is obviously not easy but the message Jesus left us in scripture is: our sensitivity to others is truly worth all the love we can put in it. I think we sense this no matter what happens. And when we are allowed to see and hear some of the workings of God that have come about during encounters with others, this truly convinces us.

One person looking back on our time together wrote to me: "And what will I leave behind from our relationship: my 'stuckness,' my unconsciousness, my shame and guilt, my repressed pain, resentment, and depression. ... And what will I take with me, what has been awakened through the gift of our relationship? My playfulness, my love of life, my sense of wonder, my gratitude, my openness, and my wholeness."

In reading her words I too was grateful. Grateful for her wonderful presence in the world and thankful to God that together we could better welcome the bright little child she had been before the abuse had crushed her initial energetic presence in the world. In addition, I was happy we could also respect the talented adult she had since begun to embrace in the past few years of our time together. The joy we could both feel now was that the abuse of long ago would not be the last word in the formation of her identity and her life. No. She was a victim no more. *Deo gratias.*

Yet, as I reflected on our time together I also recognized that in the meeting times with her (and others who turned to me to walk with them), I knew that a sensitive understanding of myself—both my sins and my talents—had helped me to recognize and appreciate a little better what I needed to say and do during these encounters and to be more of a healing, sensitive presence that could be of greater service to others.

More and more, I saw clearly how self-awareness and sensitivity to others were so entwined. Collaboration depended on this. Mutual respect was grounded in it. And I came to be more curious than ever before as to who I was on a deeper level. The travels with others made me want to travel more in search of the person God was also calling me to be.

In helping others find their "true name" I wished more than ever to find my own in life. For I recognized the more I knew about myself and was able to embrace what was really true, the more present I could be to others in an honest, helpful, and vulnerable way. And I believe this is so with all persons who wish to be sensitive persons in this harsh world. So, with this in mind, we turn now to the next section: Deep Sensitivity. For, it is in meeting God that we will ultimately find our own identity and in turn, once again, be able to be more sensitive to others—especially those in need.

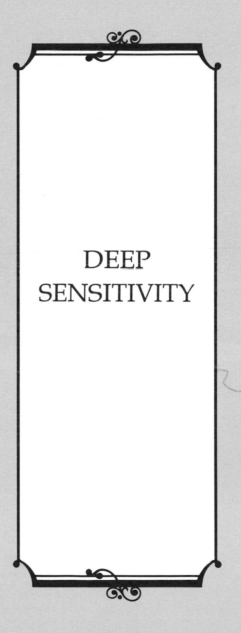

DEEP
SENSITIVITY

FIVE

"Street Spirituality"

A deep sensitivity to God is the source of all sensitivity. With an awareness of God in our lives we are able to embrace two essential truths: we are not alone and we must be sensitive to the needs of others. With God in our lives we feel integrated, centered, hopeful, loved. Without the presence of the Lord, we feel unloved, alone, and so burdened by the presence of human cruelty (including our own if we are honest) that we tend to become judgmental, passive, cynical, and periodically even to despair. At times like these, sensitivity to ourselves and others doesn't really seem very possible.

Life is very difficult and harsh at times. A person who lives a truly prayerful life—a "street spirituality"—knows this and doesn't avoid such painful realities. Instead he or she brings them to God during liturgy or community prayer, quiet periods of solitude, and in reflective moments of prayerfulness during the activity of the day.

Our joy does not come from a triumphant God who keeps us above the fray, a sullen God who says suffering is all we can expect, or a private God we hide away with from the world (although it is natural to want a God like this at times). The joy and peace of a life of prayer is in welcoming and being sensitive to a truthful and faithful God who will call, teach, save, and love us—no matter how harsh life becomes for us and others.

A deep sensitivity to God—a street spirituality—is a call for us to live in the classic tension of welcoming God into our lives both in our transformative private and communal prayer and during those times of encounter with others during the activity of our day. To avoid either side of the tension is to court either the disaster of quietism (a prayer life that is unreal and indulgent) or undisciplined activism which will only eventually lead to withdrawal and discouragement. A deep sensitivity to God is the source of our sensitivity to ourselves and others. It is in this light that this important focus is presented.

"Street Spirituality": Embracing the Classic Tension Between Prayer and Action

Early in the morning of a new beautiful Thai day, I woke up to my alarm, quickly got dressed, had several cups of strong tea, and walked over to a nearby beach with a new friend from the retreat center. We went to take a swim and pray at sunrise in what was once known as the Gulf of Siam.

In some ways it was perfect—spiritually romantic! The sun was about to rise on the calm sea and as I floated in the warm water I saw young Buddhist monks walking along the shore with full begging bowls, having successfully made their rounds to request food from respectful Thais who wished to support their quest and gain merit.

But as I continued to float I could also recognize the construction of mammoth new buildings on the beach and see the morning outlines of existing hotels that I had recently learned were pouring raw sewage directly into the Gulf. In fact, I had been warned that I was taking a chance by swimming in what was once a pristine but now quite polluted body of water.

I also knew that as the day got older, the monks who were now walking along in silence would be replaced by European and American male tourists and the women they had hired to be their sexual companions. AIDS and the sexual degradation of women would be the new afternoon reality to replace the one of respect and holiness now present on the shore.

Just as surely as the monks' saffron robes were a symbol of hope, new images that spoke of loneliness, competition, greed, hostility, and abuse of power would follow. With that thought, I recognized that if society continues to move in these destructive directions, any spirituality that would be true and real would have to take stock of such contradictions.

This leaves us with a classic tension between prayer and action. On the one hand we need a hope based on a deep faith nurtured in silent prayer; and on the other a proven faith anchored and developed in our encounters with each other. To forsake one end of the spectrum is to endanger the other. To avoid silence and solitude is to court burnout and disillusionment; yet, to foster quietism while the forests are devastated and persons are being abused due to their gender, race, ethnic, or financial state, is to let our period of so-called "spiritual solitude" become like stagnant water. It may be calm and still, but it will also be putrid, not the life-giving water of God. Real spirituality dawns only when God is as real as the problems and joys we face each day—an impossibility if we cut our prayer off from our responsibilities and daily realities.

The world is a desperate place. I see it in the faces of the abused and neglected who come for therapy and write or call for spiritual support. And I encounter it on a daily basis in the broader arena of today's news reports as well.

In one such news story a member of a relief service was walking through a section of Bosnia when he encountered a man trimming the flowers and bushes around the rubble of what used to be his home. When asked what he was doing, he simply replied that his wife and daughters had died in the building and he came each day to tend to their grave so it would be beautiful.

How can we, like this man, continue to be sensitive persons and have hope when faced with situations such as this? How can our faith stand against continuing atrocities and despair? While it is no less painful for spiritually-alive sensitive persons than for others, unlike others, we have no choice. Our faith calls us to such an attitude of firm hope.

That hope must be based on concrete encounters with God in silence and solitude. Otherwise, the despair that is sold on TV every morning and in the newspapers every evening will surely win out. It is only when we are reminded of the duplicity in our own hearts that we avoid the dangers of harshly criticizing others as charlatans. It is only when we see our response to pain as being part of God's overall response, which includes the prayer of others as well, that we can see in our aloneness with God that we are never really alone.

This, however, is only one part of the equation. Although solitude and praying in silence are a part of following Jesus' example, it must also include sensitive intimacy with others. Time alone with God is not meant to replace the communal sense of God that is experienced when two or more are gathered in the Lord's name. We recognize that our quiet reflection must be tempered and needs to be fired by interactions in which we are open, vulnerable, and looking for God beyond our projections and needs. Street Spirituality then is the place where contemplation and action meet.

None of this is new of course, but the need for generosity—in how we embrace God's gifts to us in contemplation and action—may be needed now more than ever before. If we are honest, this presents us with a problem. Once again, sensitivity to others and compassion sound wonderful in the abstract, but concrete love is another story. When faced with misery and pain, no matter what our intentions, there is certainly a temptation to pull back and sit, rationalizing that it is enough to take care of our own needs. Running and hiding are natural responses to anxiety, no matter how good a person we claim to be. Being cut off from trouble, though, will never completely shield us from having to face our vulnerability, limitations, and mortality. We owe it to ourselves and those who follow us to face life with a serious sense of honesty. And part of this honesty must include a willingness to look at why we—including those of us who proclaim to be committed to ministry—seem to avoid embracing a full life of prayer today.

Why People Don't Pray: Recognizing and Resolving Resistances to a Life of Prayer

French novelist George Sand once said: "Wisdom ... teaches us to see something outside ourselves that is higher than what is within us, and gradually, through contemplation and admiration, to come to resemble it."[1] For many, prayer is a beautiful midwife to the birth of such wisdom. If this is so, why do we talk more about prayer than actually entering into prayer where an ongoing intimate relationship with God can grow?

When I started seeing persons in therapy who are engaged in full-time ministry, I thought as a realist I would find out from them that prayer in silence and solitude each day would be a rarity. Much to my surprise the situation was even worse. Prayer for most of them—even though they claimed that God was at the center of their lives and hopes—was not a rarity, it was an oddity!

Since these persons were good, intelligent, dedicated, compassionate, and in many ways holy individuals, I wondered why they would avoid a life of prayer which would help them to be more sensitive to God so they could in turn be more sensitive to themselves and others? I decided to delve further into my own resistance as well as the experiences and comments of others who were religious. I wanted the answer to this question in their lives as well.

The first thing one encounters is a set of stock answers: "I'm too busy." "I put it off and then forget to do it during the day or at night." "I used to pray but have gotten out of the habit." Or, "My life is my prayer." But there seem to be other sources of resistances worth discussing here. They include:

1) Lack of familiarity,

2) Boredom,

3) Avoidance of shame,

4) Failure to see results,

5) Inappropriate use of sacred scripture,

6) Fear,

7) Inability to see the role of love,

8) Desire to control,

9) Attachment,

10) Lack of connection with daily activities and challenges.

1. Lack of Familiarity

Thomas Merton, the Catholic contemplative, knew that the usefulness of guidance for people desiring to find God in prayer was at best a shaky process. He felt people were always in over their heads in prayer and that persons need to develop their own spiritual compass; magnetic north is different depending on who you are, what your circumstances are, and in what interpersonal setting you live.

When pressed to offer a way to God in prayer, James Finley offered the metaphor of a field of untrodden snow in which one is looking for a path. He said: "Where is the path? The answer is to walk across it and there will be a path."[2]

For many, moving ahead in such darkness with a lack of certainty takes stamina and faith. With one older brother who was complaining of a loss of will to persevere, Merton simply counseled: "Courage comes and goes; hold on for the next supply."[3]

For others the problem is one of looking in the wrong place or in a familiar way for God that doesn't produce adequate results any more. The following admission of Henri

Nouwen, which contains the advice of Abbot John Eudes Bamberger, illustrates this point:

> I had the fantasy that one day God just might break through the hard shell of my resistance and reveal himself to me in such an intensive and convincing way that I would be able to let my "idols" go and commit myself unreservedly to him. John Eudes was not too surprised by the fantasy and said, "You want God to appear to you in the way your passions desire, but these passions make you blind to his presence now. Focus on the nonpassionate part of yourself and realize God's presence there. Let that part grow in you and make your decision from there. You will be surprised to see how powers that seem invincible shrivel away.[4]

Consequently, the unfamiliar must become our friend in prayer, the unspoken must offer God's words, and the vague be a place for something new in our hearts to be formed which can be lived out in the concrete with others. I think we can take solace and encouragement too from Thomas Aldrich who says in his work *Leaves from a Notebook*: "I like to have a thing suggested rather than told in full. When every detail is given the mind rests satisfied, and the imagination loses the desire to use its own wings."[5]

It is in such prayer that dreams, a curriculum of the heart, can be formed anew with broad brush strokes of the unfamiliar. In Proverbs we read that when people don't have a dream, they dry up, disappear, or run the risk of embracing a false dream fired by secularism's desire for power, fame, security, money, satisfaction, knowledge, respect, and happiness. All of these things in themselves may be good, but when they become our ultimate and overriding goal in life then we have lost our freedom.

Take as an example the Sunday magazine of the *New York Times*. The dreams and promises of peace and joy offered us by the ads there certainly outweigh the principles and ethics expounded by the beautiful but unfortunately less powerful articles on poverty, justice, and the value of education that accompany them. If we don't have a sensitivity to this reality, others will supply our images and the narrow gate which leads to the possibility of real dreams of joy and peace will be temporarily blocked.

The prayer of the unfamiliar allows us to be more sensitive to the living God. It is designed to break through not only the crust of our self-satisfaction, but also through the seduction of the idols that surround us and are ready to fill the vacuum left by the temporary absence of the images and knowledge which comes to us in a prayer of silence (so we can listen to God) and solitude (so we can be with God).

I remember once seeing a little saying on a plaque in front of a beautiful flower bed: "There is always music in the garden amongst the trees. But your heart must be silent to hear it." This is the silence of patience and wonder which we set aside when we abandon our prayer because we feel foolish in our silent quiet presence to God. And this is the very resistance we are called to recognize and gently put aside in prayer with God's help.

2. Boredom

In therapy when I treat people involved in full-time ministry, I often ask them to tell me a bit about their prayer life. What they usually say is that they don't contemplate much now. I ask them to describe how they do pray and what the content of their prayer is. When they are done, I often think to myself: "No wonder they don't pray. It sounds so boring, if I were them I would avoid it too."

In her book *The Rehearsal* Jean Anouilh poses the question: "Have you noticed that life, real, honest-to-goodness life, with murders and catastrophes and fabulous inheritances, happens almost exclusively in the newspapers?"[6] I think the same can be said of our prayer life. We read about the vibrant prayer life of others in spiritual books and sit wistfully wondering why ours can't be that way. Often we mistakenly decide the reason for this is our lack of holiness or our inexperience with the techniques of prayer.

Yet, this is far from the truth. For just as Jesus came to heal sinners, the Spirit he bequeathed to us is here for those of us who are lost. The real issue, which we may not even have begun to grasp, is one that I have had to emphasize again and again, with myself and others. Real spirituality dawns when God becomes as real as the problems and joys we face each day.

Often the problem is that our prayer is too artificial, bland, and compartmentalized. If our prayer is dull, we must then ask ourselves when was the last time we spoke with God about things that really mattered to us in our daily lives?

Do we share our angers, joys, impulses, secrets, addictions, and anxieties? Do we talk to the Lord about our perversions, desires, needs, resistances, and failures? For instance, when have we last said to God: "I love you," "Down deep, I doubt you exist," or "I hate the way you are running this world!!"

Where is the passion? Rabbi Lionel Blue used to say that Jews are not holy asparagus growing up to the heavens. Instead, he noted that Jews are noisy. They grapple with God.[7] If we really believe we are in covenant with God too, shouldn't we be doing this as well?

Often I will be with a group of people who are talking and one of them will finally call the meeting to order and begin to lead a short prayer using a voice that doesn't sound like his own at all. When this happens I irreverently think to myself: "If God responds to this prayer it will be to someone who actually owns this voice and lives in Peoria. She will be getting the blessings and he will wonder why God didn't hear his request."

If God is to be real, if our faith is to be real, then our prayer must be real and include everything. Everything. If we are hesitant to speak about masturbation, then we fail to recognize that God made us and knows how all the parts work. If we are afraid to speak about such things as our pettiness, embarrassing moments, tendency to act only when we are very secure, our addictions, the anger that sits below our veneer of "chronic niceness," or the lies we are involved in living, then how can we take the first step toward dealing with them? How can we admit that we are helpless and at present not willing to change? Such honesty is the very essences of a thrilling life of prayer. How can we be sensitive to God and expect God to be sensitive to us if we are artificial in our presentation of who we are?

3. Not Wanting to Challenge Our Shame

Kahlil Gibran wrote in one of his lesser known works *Sand and Foam*: "Should we all confess our sins to one another we would all laugh at one another for our lack of originality."[8] Although this is so, we resist looking at our sins and failings because we believe they prove that we are people who should not be appreciated and loved. Jean-Jacques Rousseau recognizes this in his *Confessions* when he says: "It is not the criminal things which are the hardest to confess, but the ridiculous and shameful."[9]

When we meet people who sensitively embrace the truth as easily as they do all other parts of reality it surprises us. Their simplicity and direct sense of what is and what isn't throws us off guard; we just don't know what to say.

In Thailand I met several people like this and heard stories about still others. While for many people and cultures truth is a hazy commodity and facts are things to be ignored or hoarded, these people share "private" information like we share comments on the weather.

In Chiang Mai in the north of Thailand I got into a taxi on the way to the mountain temple Doi Su Tep. After we were driving along for five minutes the driver pointed to a hospital we were passing. He said, "I work there too," and he told us what he earned both there and as a taxi driver. He then asked: "Where do you work and what do you earn?"

People visiting Thailand are often surprised if they are noticeably overweight. Since the Thais have the gift of being able to eat constantly and not gain weight, they wonder about the phenomenon out loud when they meet heavy people. And so, it is not unusual for a heavy person to be greeted in a department store or taxi with the question: "How did you get so fat?" It's not that they are prejudiced against persons who are heavy. It's just that they are intrigued, honest, and direct. After all, if something is so, why would one want to deny it?

The real clincher for me was a story shared by a member of an international relief agency working in the very south of Thailand. She said she was sitting with her morning coffee, half-asleep and musing about the fact she was soon going to be transferred to France, when she overheard a discussion between a cook and housekeeper for the agency. They were trying to decide on how to differentiate between two new men in the house, both named Bill.

Finally, the relief worker heard them confidently proclaim that they were going to call one of the workers "Bill the Handsome" and the other "Bill the Ugly." Upon hearing this, she almost spilled her coffee over her blouse and immediately went in to the kitchen to speak with them about it.

She apologized for overhearing their conversation, but said to them that they couldn't do what they were planning because both Bills understood Thai. In response to this the cook and housekeeper looked puzzled. The cook said: "What's the difference if they understand Thai?"

She answered: "Well, what if the one who you are calling 'Bill the Ugly' overhears you? He will be terribly upset."

To which the cook responded: "You mean he doesn't know?"

Although we may not be as direct—or want to be—with others in our own culture, we do have to be blunt with ourselves and with God in prayer otherwise we will miss much. The truth brings with it so much more freedom and vision than either ignorance or a "varnished" view of reality does. William Blake in "The Marriage of Heaven and Hell" states: "A fool sees not the same tree that a wise man sees."[10] The question we have to ask ourselves is whether we are trying to be wise without being truthful. If so, then we are on a never ending treadmill which will circle us through episodes of hidden relief and anxious pain. We will live in fear of being discovered for who or what we are, not wanting to face ourselves or allowing others to see us.

In prayer, when we challenge our shame before a loving God, our sins come to light and we recognize that we are not the same as our sins. We see again the difference between guilt which results from admitting I've *done* something wrong and shame which is produced by the pervading erroneous belief that I *am* someone wrong.

To break through the chains of shame so we can take our place in the world, the hidden elements of sin must come to the surface, be faced, and shared with a loving God who tells us, "Go and sin no more." I guess the old saying is valid: "The truth will set you free ... but first it will make you miserable." However, this temporary misery is a small price to pay for the freedom that comes with realizing that we are known and loved by God.

Being a friend of God helps us to see we don't need an image for others. And it saves us energy, because the energy we don't use on self-protection can be spent on sensitivity, openness, and creativity. This then transfers over into our life giving us energy there for growth and relationship.

4. We Don't See Results in the Usual Ways

There is a Zen saying I quoted earlier that advises: "Face reality and unwilled change will take place." In prayer, as we stand naked before God, there is a movement in our unconscious attitude that we may not notice that results in our relating to ourselves and others in a more free way. It is a basic and beautiful fruit of true prayer. The psychological reason for this is that when our attitude is healthy, our actions will naturally be good without our even having to think about them.

Likewise, prayer also produces changes that we may not see directly in our environment but which make all the difference in life. One bishop shared with his priests and the people of his diocese that he really didn't know whether the prayers he was saying made any difference, but he did know one thing: when he stopped praying, many good things seemed to stop as well. This is a point worth keeping in mind since society trains us to look for results in certain ways. This can lead to discouragement when we don't see things happen at the time and in the way we want.

A secular devotion to action which disdains the goodness and immeasurable value of contemplation can also keep us from valuing the time for prayer, especially during those periods when we are involved in doing things we consider good and important. As a result we may feel fulfilled by our visible impact but still question whether what we have done is really God's will.

Rabbi Abraham Joshua Heschel, a well-known religious figure of his time, knew the importance of action but was well aware of the danger of trying to root action in the shallow soil of a life without prayer. As much as he saw ethics as something to be lived rather than taught, his approach was also balanced by a sense of the Sabbath and a reverential respect for the necessity of quiet time in solitude with God.

One day during the period when the Second Vatican Council was in session (at which Heschel was an invited official observer), Heschel encountered a Catholic priest who taught and wrote about spirituality. After speaking with him for a few moments, he invited him to come home with him for refreshments and a visit.

As they walked together, the priest said to Abraham Heschel: "Rabbi, pardon my comment, but you seem somewhat sad." To this comment Heschel nodded affirmatively. The priest then asked: "What was it that made you sad?" To which the rabbi responded: "My morning prayer made me sad." Undaunted, the priest pushed him further with the question: "What about your morning prayer made you sad Rabbi?"

Rabbi Heschel stopped on the sidewalk, turned to the priest and said: "Let me ask you a question, Father. How many of your bishops at the Council are contemplatives?" At which point, the priest later reported: "Then I became sad."

Heschel was able to see that action—even essential action in support of the good—without quiet, reflective sensitivity to God was dangerous. Prayer and *mitzvot* (good action) are both part of a mystical appreciation of life. Maybe this is why Henri Nouwen believes that silence and solitude are the furnace in which transformation takes place and results in deeds of love rather than actions prompted by compulsion and guilt.[11]

It is easy to miss the opportunity to develop our prayer life and to deepen our relationship with the Lord because our day is too full of other good things. Once when I was speaking with my spiritual director about prayer he recognized that while I was valuing the importance of having my work be a prayerful experience, I was also missing an important element. If I continued to miss it, the opportunities I would be given to deepen my relationship with, and sensitivity to the true, living God might be jeopardized.

He said: "Well, of course you are right to see prayer in the broad context of things and appreciate your work and leisure as forms of worship. However, some caution might be important here. You see, when you receive the grace to pray during the day, there may be a temptation during this period to go and do something else. You may make a phone call and it may be a good thing that you are doing. You may go read a book and that may be beneficial as well. However, when you are done with these actions, the grace to pray, meet, and get to know God in silence and solitude may be temporarily gone as well. So, be attuned to the graces you are given for different things including prayer and try—in God's rhythm—to respond accordingly." I think this is very good advice.

5. Inappropriate or Inadequate Use of Scripture

In prayer we often feel lost because our God is too vague and our understanding of the history of relationships between God and the human person is either almost absent or too intellectual. Unfortunately, religious people are sometimes the worst persons with respect to scripture reading because it is not new for them. They know how all the stories end up!

Once a young man approached the famous Rebbe Israel Baal Shem Tov and asked how he might become a rabbi. The Rebbe sent him away with the advice that he seriously read Torah. In several months the young man was already back. Upon his return he quickly uttered with confidence: "Rebbe, I have been through Torah ten times." To which the Rebbe responded quietly and gently: "Yes, but how many times has Torah been through you?"

In the fourth and fifth century deserts of Persia and northern Africa, the Ammas and Abbas of the period who were known for their prayer which had scripture at the heart of it. Both Kenneth Leech and Thomas Merton remind us of this from different vantage points, but to the same end:

> The Desert Fathers held, with Epiphanius of Cyprus, that "ignorance of the Scriptures is a precipice and a deep abyss." They used the psalms constantly. Their prayer was utterly and profoundly biblical. The contemplation of God was inseparable from the response to God's word in revelation, and the deep, inner struggle with the heart invoked in the interiorizing and digesting of the Scriptures.[12]
>
> Prayer was the very heart of the desert life, and consisted of psalmody (vocal prayer—recitation of the Psalms and other parts of the Scriptures which everyone had to know by heart) and contemplation. What we would call today contemplative prayer is referred to as *quies* or "rest." This illuminating term has persisted in Greek monastic tradition as *hesychia*, "sweet repose." *Quies* is a silent absorption aided by the soft repetition of a lone phrase of the Scriptures....[13]

When we encounter sacred scripture with sensitivity and a sense of energy, the persons in the stories become friends with whom we can almost converse, and themes from the Bible become places for us to test our identity and reflect on our way of living. This results in a change in our prayer and life.

A good indicator of this is when scripture can mentally bubble up to the surface of the rough seas of our daily problems to help us gain perspective and have courage. Prayer doesn't replace scripture; it is a new page in it. Therefore, a simple regimen of reading scriptures for their own sake, not as part of a religious service, for study, or homily preparation is essential. Sensitivity to God includes, first and foremost, a radical sensitivity to the word God has given us in sacred scriptures.

6. Fear

There is a proverb from Cameroon that reads: "He who asks the questions cannot avoid the answers." Persons who have encountered God in prayer have discovered this in surprising ways. Certainly, as we read the spiritual classics or the comments of recent religious figures, we see it in their words.

Two of my favorite of the more classic and well-known statements that reflect the fear that is part of encounter with the living God are from Paul Tillich and Metropolitan Anthony of Sourozh (Anthony Bloom). Paul Tillich said: "If you've never run away from your God, I wonder who your God is."[14] Metropolitan Anthony echoes these sentiments in his now famous and often quoted claim that to meet God is like entering the cave of the tiger. The image he gives is that the encounter with God is not like meeting a pussycat but a tiger. For him, the realm of God is dangerous.[15]

Part of this realm is the setting of silence and solitude. In contemplation persons wait to meet God, but forget that in doing this they are clearing out their consciousness and creating a psychological vacuum. When this is done it leaves room for the preconscious to rise and with it the denials, lies, self-deceit, and games we have played to distort or avoid the truth.

Rather than avoiding this reality, it is important for us to accept the difficulty it poses. As Thomas Merton reminds us: "It is in the unconscious that true purification and repentance have to reach down and happen."[16] It forms the basis of an orientation toward hope, and a gentle but strong sensitivity to the place of love in our lives.

To open our arms to God, we must stop holding onto the things which may give us illusory security now. We have heard people talk about this *ad infinitum* and maybe *ad nauseam*, but to actually experience it is something quite different.

The best way I have to understand it is related to something that occurred to me many years ago. I have related this briefly in other writings, but it is worth repeating more fully here. It was the first time that I had a patient going through what is often referred to as the "working through" phase of psychotherapy. In this phase, the patient comes to a point where the heart and the head come together and produce change. Some people think that understanding is the source of change, but it really isn't. If an alcoholic comes in to see me, and I help the person gain understanding, all I have on my hands is an enlightened alcoholic. Nothing has really changed in terms of behavior and attitude. However, when the heart and head come together, change begins to happen.

In the case I mentioned, the person coming in to see me had problems with spontaneously being herself. She was handcuffed with a veneer of chronic niceness. She always tried to please people because she was frightened of rejection and had low self-esteem. As we moved through therapy, she began to interact more freely with me until she reached the point where she seemed to be able to relate without giving it much thought. She would even tease me occasionally and felt at ease to question my interpretations (which in a number of instances proved to be crucial, because I was quite off the mark.)

Yet, when she began to apply her insights to relationships in the outside world she seemed to regress and play her old pleasing games again. Puzzled by this, I asked her why she seemed to act one way with me and another with friends, family, and acquaintances. She quickly replied: "Don't you understand? I trust you. In here it is like the light is on and I can see where I am going. Out there it is dark and I fear if I am simply myself and respond as I think fit, the results may be terrible. It is like there is a pit out there and I fear falling into it with feelings of shame and vulnerability."

These words reminded me of something I had encountered when in the military. I had forgotten all about it. (As a matter of fact, for some reason I had forgotten about the whole three years in the service! … I wonder why?) The scene was the confidence course—a terrible series of obstacles to be surmounted within a short span of time. The person in charge was standing next to me, dressed something like a Boy Scout but with a round brown hat like Smokey the Bear. I shared my hesitance and implied that I might best sit it out at this point so I didn't hold everyone up.

He gave me an incredulous look and whispered something in my ear. Now, given the type of book this is I won't repeat exactly what he said. But to give you some sense of it, my response was: "Is what you just suggested anatomically possible?"

He responded quickly with: "I'll show you if you don't get moving!" To which I quickly added: "You know, I'm feeling new motivation welling up within me!"

As I went through the series of obstacles I came to the middle of the course and saw what I thought was an easy task compared to the other ones. It was a small A-frame made of logs, with a rope hanging from it and a small ditch underneath. I thought to myself: "I have these Marines all wrong. This is a confidence builder. How good of them to give us a break in this way."

However, I noticed that the big fellows in front of me, who compared to my small stature seemed to be almost seven feet tall, couldn't seem to do it. They would swing over and then swing back. Some would swing over, get their feet down, let go of the rope and fall back into the ditch, scrambling for the rope to save themselves.

I couldn't figure out what the problem was. The Drill Instructor had no problem doing the obstacle and yet he was much smaller than they were. Finally it hit me.

There was only one way you could pass this obstacle. You had to run as fast as you could, grab the rope, swing over and in midair, let go. If you tried to wait until you were on solid ground it was already too late.

The same can be said not only of the "working through" phase of therapy, but also of prayer. Deep sensitivity to God is a faithful leap into the darkness. Where it leads no one really knows, but too much concern about safety at various points in prayer is an impediment that all but stops us from reaching sacred ground.

7. Inability to See the Role of Love

Gertrude Mueller Nelson in her book *Here All Dwell Free* wrote:

> Romantic love is not an aberration, it is heady stuff that launches ships and makes the world go round. It is a powerful taste of the divine as we experience it in one another. It is also the necessary vision that allows one to be crazy and daring enough to make a commitment.[17]

The irony is that even though prayer is by its very definition an act of love and a recognition of being loved, sometimes love is not as present as it should be. The result is that prayer becomes a dutiful act, or the enactment of techniques.

Most of us are "closet Pelagians" at some time or other. We think that we can gain heaven or pray properly with our own skills and by our own efforts. We fail to recognize that while discipline and methods of prayer may be helpful, prayer is first and foremost a relationship based on love: ours and God's.

Contemplation is also first and foremost a gift. It involves the freedom of God as well as our own initiatives. Consequently, one of the first questions we need to ask ourselves in prayer is about the attitude with which we are entering the relationship. If it is with the respect, humility, and awe that are part of love of the Divine, then we are coming to the encounter with a proper sense of the depth involved.

But if it is just with a sense of obligation, that we ought to be there, then the result will be one of frustration, like a hide-and-seek game with a God whom we are not even sure is interested in us.

The famous psychiatrist Karl Menninger once surprised his technique and theory-oriented colleagues with the simple statement: "Love is a medicine for the sickness of the world; a prescription often given, rarely taken."[18] Just as this is true for the world, love is also the basic prescription for prayer life that is ill and limping.

Without love there is little passion in our sensitivity to God's presence in our life. And without fire in prayer, there is little motivation to continue. The result is periods when prayer is dull or absent. The question we must ask about our prayer is: "Where is the passion?" It may be a nice time we spend alone thinking about God, but it lacks the drama and intensity of true prayer.

I don't mean that prayer has to lead to special feelings of warmth or inspiration. Leaving prayer with a deep sense of cognitive clarity is sometimes passionate. However, when technique becomes paramount rather than supportive, and the deep love of intensity and awareness is not present, prayer becomes just another activity, and not such a joyous one.

In one of his final presentations on prayer, Anthony de Mello said we must ask: "Where is the fire?" He told a story something like this to make his point.

Once there was a man who invented fire. He was a good man and wished to share it with others. He first went to one village and showed them how to make fire. They were very grateful for it, but did not get a chance to thank him because he left early one morning without their seeing him. He did not need to be thanked. He was a great man and this was not important to him.

He then went to another village and began to teach them how to make fire, but the village shamans were not happy about this. They could see he was taking power from them and was a danger to their position among the people. They plotted to kill him but wanted to do it without the people suspecting their involvement.

So, they quietly poisoned him before he could show the people how they could make fire themselves. And after he was found dead, made a great show of concern about his death. One of the ways they did this was by developing a ritual in which respect would be shown to the man who invented fire. They built an altar and put around it the implements the man had used to make fire.

They gathered the people daily to say his name, show gratitude for his presence, and to see the tools he had used. But, there was no fire.[19]

His point was without fire there is no real prayer. The difference between a prayer life with real fire, light, and warmth, and one in which we talk or think about fire but act in ways which show that true passion is missing is that in the latter the heart of a real relationship with God is also absent. The question again is: "Where's the passion? Where's the fire?"

8. Desire to Control

We hear people speak about "the adventure of a life of prayer." Yet, there is resistance to opening ourselves in our sensitivity to the Spirit because it involves the risk of surrendering control. Ralph Waldo Emerson noted: "All life is an experiment. The more experiments you make, the better." But rather than a life marked by "experiments" or a willingness to jump into the dark, we live lives of rhythm and habit which tosses us between tension and anomie.

In psychotherapy patients risk interacting with someone who doesn't fit the patterns of other people in their lives. When they try to transfer onto the therapist an image of someone from their early years and behave as if the therapist were that person, the therapist reflects it back onto them so they can see that they are projecting such an image. Although this is ultimately freeing for the patient, in the interim before they work through the transference, they are frightened to have this person "loose in their psyche"—one whom they cannot pin down, pigeonhole, or categorize and then react to accordingly.

They find it difficult to deal with someone who is generous, but not overly solicitous; firm, but not rejecting; honest, yet not hurtful; accepting, but not afraid to point to unpleasant behaviors and addictions.

The same can be said with respect to a sensitive prayer life—but to the ultimate degree! We fear risking the presence of the Spirit in our lives in a way which ends in our not being able to control God's presence or message. We say we want the love of the relationship, but often we finish the sentence under our breath with "in our way and on our terms."

Once again, there is no bargaining with freedom. Either the relationship is real and open, or it isn't. And if it isn't, then prayer suffers accordingly.

9. Uncovering Attachments

Abbot John Eudes Bamberger once said: "If you cannot be detached from all you do and like to do, you cannot live a full spiritual life."[20] But often in the course of the day we are surrounded by voices that drown out the recognition of our attachments. What the world considers wonderful is often reinforced by TV, our friends, the books we read, and the news we deem worthy. But it may not be in our best interest.

This is obviously not a recent phenomenon. In Jeremiah 22:21 we read: "I spoke to you in your prosperity, but you said: 'I will not listen.'" Nor, is a fact to be taken lightly or easily dismissed as being an example of dualism (a separation of the world and the spirit). When we are sensitive this reality comes to light in prayer. We slowly but surely recognize the voices of culture which emphasize financial security, entitlement, self-reliance, competition, power, success, and extreme individualism and we realize that they don't seem as valid anymore.

In true prayer, our idols come to light and we see how we really prefer the darkness where we don't have to face them. We begin to see a glimmer of our denials and avoidances; we begin to recognize the buds of spiritual self-awareness which we can pray over and share with others.

Puzzlement, for instance, may be the initial flowering of a recognition of what we are attached to in life. In my case, I couldn't figure out why I was so interested in buying, furnishing, and landscaping a new house while at the same time felt I could move in a minute. I wondered why I would really like to buy a used Jaguar, but felt I could sell it a month afterward. What was I attached to with respect to these two things? I discussed it with my wife and she replied: "It is not the things (car, house …) you are attached to as much as the concept, what they represent for you (i.e., success, power, attractiveness …)." Hearing this was helpful because I could then bring it back to prayer.

Other attachments are easier to note. We can just look at ourselves and our preoccupations. For instance, if we are heavy—even taking into consideration our metabolism rate—maybe it is food. In such cases, a diet and some exercise might be a desert experience we would want to avoid but should embrace. In other cases, it might be work, success (ours or the achievements of our children, religious order, church, or denomination), comfort, need to control or organize, travel, stimulation, alcohol, our image—the list is endless.

Something that has helped me and I have suggested to others as a way to uncover their attachments is the simple question: "Who is my god?" As Jesus noted in very direct terms: "Wherever your treasure is, there will be your heart too" (Mt 6:21).

When I ask a group of religious persons this question, they often come up with many theologically-sound and spiritually-beautiful answers. But then I remind them that I am a behavioral scientist who is a strict adherent to Jesus' words. So, if someone tells me that they love me and then they drop a rock on my head, needless to say I have great doubts about the veracity of their statement!

The same can be said about the answer to the question: "Who is my god?" My feeling, given what I've just noted, is that the answer to this question is not some verbal formulation. It is contained in our behavior. So, let me give you some examples of who our god might be. Whatever we think about before we go to bed, that is our god. Whatever we think about when we get up, that is our god. Whatever preoccupies us when we are walking, driving in a car, or during the day, that is our god.

Now sometimes I get the response: "Shouldn't I worry about things? Am I expected to have my head in the clouds?" This is a natural response. But, although it may be prompted by an honest misunderstanding of my comments, it is usually fostered by some resistance and wish to avoid the point as well.

Of course you should be concerned about the people and tasks in your life. Of course it is expected that you will be compassionate, need to plan, and enjoy what is around you. However, there is a difference between sensitive compassion and inordinate worrying, between planning to do something about a problem and preoccupying yourself with it, between enjoying food, drink, or whatever, and making it the first concern in your life. For some people I think: "God forbid that they would miss a meal." For others my hope is that in trying to be supportive to their children when they are in trouble is that once they have done what they can, they are able to let go and let God take care of what needs to be done.

Attachments are forms of silent slavery that prevent us from having a sensitive, passionate spiritual life. Ironically, these passing passions prevent us from truly enjoying life spontaneously and freely. One person who was a new member in Alcoholics Anonymous said to me: "One of the reasons I entered A.A. is I realized that my fun was, in my eyes, becoming reliant on drink. I had to have a few before I left the house and make sure that they would be serving alcohol at the party I was going to that evening. Rather than being part of the fun, it was closing out much of the joy I could experience in life. Finally, I said: 'Enough of this!' and joined A.A." For every attachment put into perspective, a greater freedom and possibility of real passion is increased.

10. Lack of Connection to Daily Activities and Challenges

True prayer challenges us to be ruthless in our sensitivity to the truth in honest interactions with others, as well as in our intimate interaction with God in silence and solitude. To forget our time alone with God is to court the disaster of undisciplined activism. But to ignore the holiness of our time with others is to set the stage for quietism. The following story accurately gauges the danger of this failure to see how the incarnation lives continually in the streets of our lives.

One day a young fugitive, trying to hide himself from the enemy, entered a small village. The people were kind to him and offered him a place to stay. But when the soldiers who sought the fugitive asked where he was hiding, everyone became fearful. The soldiers threatened to burn the village unless the young man was handed over to them before dawn.

The people, not knowing what to do, went to the minister for guidance and he, torn between handing over the boy to the enemy or having the people killed, withdrew to his room and read his Bible hoping to find the answer before dawn.

After many hours, in the early morning, his eyes fell on these words: "It is better that one person dies than that the whole people be lost." Then the minister closed his Bible, called the soldiers together and told them where the boy was hidden. And after the soldiers led the fugitive away to be killed, there was a feast in the village because the minister had saved the lives of the people. But the minister did not celebrate. Overcome with deep sadness, he remained in his room.

That night an angel of the Lord came to him and asked: "What have you done?!" He said: "I handed over the fugitive to the enemy." Then the angel said: "But don't you know you have handed over the Messiah?" "How could I have known?" replied the minister anxiously. Then the angel said: "If instead of just reading your Bible, you would have also visited this man just once and looked into his eyes, you would have known."[21]

Conclusion

Obviously, there are no easy roads into the street spirituality of which we are so in need of today. That is a reality. But simple faithfulness to prayer and action—though not easy, spectacular, or seemingly revolutionary enough—will bring with it a deep sensitivity, perspective, and direction. Like the headlights on a car, these virtues will offer enough light for us to discern the next step.

A dedication to balancing quiet reflection, involvement, and action will help us accept the contradictions and mystery of living out a street spirituality in today's world. It will help us to be sensitive enough to uncover a blueprint for living, loving, and working. This is especially needed in a world which seems so lost, so intent on steeling itself against our self-awareness and sharing of gifts and burdens of life with each other—at a time when healing interactions are most needed. Such a commitment to prayer and action in the midst of so much confusion and darkness today will lead us to experience the promise Jesus made to us so many, many years ago: "I shall not leave you orphans; I shall come to you" (Jn 14:18). And, what more can we ask of the Lord than that?

SIX

Piercing
the Darkness

At times, being a sensitive person can be a precarious undertaking. Looking at today's world sometimes feels like standing in the middle of a field and seeing a summer storm quickly gathering in the distance. You can see a black wall of rain smoothly sweeping toward you, but you're not sure what to do.

Staying in the middle of the field is not safe, if it is an electrical storm. And even if it isn't, you know by standing still you certainly will wind up getting soaked. Should you run for cover under a tree close by you might stay dry but if lightning hits the tree you may also end up dead. And, if you seek protection in a safe place down the road, you might never make it in time. None of the options seem sensible or attractive.

Trying not to think about it—and doing nothing—is certainly not the answer either. Yet, many of us feel we are in such an impasse as we face the daily despair reported on TV and in the newspapers, hear over the phone from our family, friends, and neighbors, and even personally experience in our own hearts more often than we probably would like to admit.

Somehow it seems more difficult today than ever before not to be drowned by the darkness. Maybe it isn't, but it certainly seems that way. Many of us are constantly involved in crisis management in our homes, neighborhoods, and the world, with only small respites or periods of impasse which may be without intense pain, but are still devoid of a feeling of direction or peace. Consequently, if we are to be sensitive people in contemporary life, there is a special need now to secure time each day to reflect "theologically." We need to look at our behavior, thoughts, and feelings during the day and remember what we believe.

Rather than giving in to the natural tendencies to avoid the darkness that we experience in our own hearts and the world at large, facing it is of great value in these times. While we may not be able to prevent life's storm from chilling our soul, we must do what we can. And if it is being done in the correct spirit, it will join us with others seeking to do the right thing and, of ultimate importance, it will join us with the living God who is the source of real peace, our peace. Once again, a deep sensitivity to God is at the source of a sensitivity to ourselves and others—even when, maybe especially when, there seems to be so much darkness present.

Unnecessary Darkness

The darkness we experience in life often tells just as much about us as it does about what we feel is its cause. In some cases, what it does reveal is that the darkness we encounter is really unnecessary if we are willing to be more honest from the start in our sensitivity to ourselves.

Some people always seem to be making trouble for themselves. With such moody individuals it seems as though every third Tuesday marks the arrival of yet another "dark night of the soul." (In such cases the real darkness is usually experienced by those of us who have to live with such people!) However, in less extreme cases—which hopefully is the category in which you and I fit—there is also a need to recognize that many of our problems are of our own making. This will keep us from trivializing the significant spiritual experience which John of the Cross and others have referred to as "darkness" and at the same time help us see the psychological/physical symptoms of "depression."

Much of what we face that we find dark and difficult unfortunately is partly of our own doing in this world. Yoda, the wisdom figure or "Jedi Master," made this point in the movie *The Empire Strikes Back* from the *Star Wars* trilogy that was so popular in the 1980s. In this movie, Yoda urged Luke Skywalker, the young man who was his disciple, to enter a cave that seemed to emanate danger and fear. When young Luke asked Yoda: "What's in the cave?" his simple response was: "Only what you bring in with you."

The same can be said of us as we enter "the cave of the tiger" in prayer and reflection. Many things from a myriad of sources will tear at us. But chief among them are our interior demons. They include for many of us such things as:

- Lack of self-awareness, self-acceptance, and self-love,
- Dishonesty,
- Intolerance of others,
- Unfinished business with family and friends,
- Suppressed/repressed negative feelings,
- Poorly-developed ethics, beliefs, and values,
- Attachments or addictions,
- Hidden, past, or unintegrated embarrassments,
- Resistance to intimacy,
- Failure to take care of oneself physically,
- Lack of honesty and openness in prayer,
- Lack of meaning in life,
- Ungrieved losses,
- Greed,
- Unreasonable expectations of self and others,
- A sense of entitlement,
- Undealt with anger,
- Unwillingness to risk and an inordinate need for security,

- Inability to experience quiet in one's life,
- Unhealthy self-involvement or, at the other extreme, lack of healthy self-interest,
- Failure to set priorities in life,
- Irresponsibility,
- Being overly perfectionistic and inordinately self-critical,
- Unwillingness to accept love except in ways one has predetermined as meaningful ("If _____ doesn't love me; then the other warmth and acceptance in my life isn't important."),
- Fear of responsibility and a tendency to project blame.

The darkness of a true encounter with self can be like a "psychological mirror" that crisply reflects those partially-hidden and disguised parts of our personality that keep us chained to a spirituality which isn't open or mature enough. It reflects our own rigid defenses, personal immaturities, unresolved repressed issues, hidden motivations, tenacious defenses, erroneous (yet comfortable) self-definitions, and our chameleon-like behaviors. In essence, it confronts us with the darkness of our unintegrated self.

What then does this experience of darkness call us to do? I think it calls us to take steps to live life differently. It invites us to shape a life where we can approach both God and ourselves with a greater sensitivity. We can face both our darkness and our joy with a healthier sense of self and a more responsible, honest style of relating.

I would like to outline four areas of focus where I think it might be particularly helpful for us to take steps toward honest sensitivity with self, God, and others. We need to cultivate a:

- Willingness to review basic ways in which we can be more responsible psychologically in how we live in general,
- Method to uncover our own spiritual theology,

- Process for reflecting theologically each day on how we are living,
- Practical method for discerning God's call to us in life and an awareness of how we can best be involved in this process.

Being Psychologically Responsible

To be responsible psychologically is one of the best ways we can set the stage for *metanoia* (conversion) in our own lives and in the sensitive involvement we have with others. You can't share with others what you don't have. If you try to give sensitively to others the end result is often a compulsive offering of self, usually terminating in burnout and disillusionment.

Being psychologically responsible involves at least informally addressing a number of areas in our lives and reflecting on the ones which seem to be problematic. The temptation of course is to avoid recognition of a problem or to push it aside by noting: "Oh, I guess I should do something about this issue. It has been a problem for years with me."

In doing this it seems like we are addressing the difficulty but we are merely acknowledging it quickly in a way that really says: "Now that I have said something about it, everything is all right again. I'll just act in the same way until someone brings it up or it becomes obvious again."

Instead, we need to review our lives on a periodic basis so avoidance and denial don't take root and sprout to block self-awareness. With this in mind, the following "check list" of psychological health is meant to help foster personal sensitivity and better dialogue with ourselves (and possibly someone who is trusted by us). Such increased personal sensitivity and better dialogue can lead to a plan of action to address the issue we have—including surfacing aspects in ourselves that need to be prayed about so we can move closer to God through our honest sensitivity and a firmer recognition of the need for grace.

Psychological Health Checklist

1) *Attention to physical health:* Rest, diet, and activity (leisure/work) are elements which rely on our attitude. Are we balancing them? Are we getting enough sleep, eating too much or sporadically, drinking alcohol to an excess, active enough to allow for sufficient oxygen exchange in the body?

2) *Assertiveness—not passivity or aggression:* Are we aware of our feelings and beliefs, and do we present them to others in a timely, appropriate fashion?

3) *Values and meaning:* Are we aware of our ethics in how we live? Is this translated into our prioritization of activities, into the willingness to risk vulnerability with others? Do our actions reflect what we believe and value? Do we avoid overburdening ourselves so we can't do what we choose with a sense of attentiveness?

4) *Self-awareness:* Do we have times during the day when we are able to look at our thoughts, feelings, and behavior in a curious and constructive fashion? Or, do we avoid thinking about our lives, or only stop to occasionally condemn ourselves?

5) *Acceptance of love and criticism:* Are we willing to accept, rather than devalue, the love that is already around us? Are we also willing to accept criticism rather than projecting the blame onto others, or constantly being angry, sarcastic, or unduly hypersensitive?

6) *Creative ways in relating to others:* Do we emphasize only one style of interacting with others or are we willing to entertain such varying approaches as: being more direct, having greater patience, standing aside, confronting, accepting? Do we look for ways to change the goals when our primary style doesn't seem indicated or is not working very well?

7) *"Soft power":* Are we willing to see and act upon the value of such traits as gentleness, imagination, relaxation, active listening, retreat, and patience? Do we model them in situations where others may benefit from it?

8) *Cognition:* Do we take the time to plan, prioritize, and review our habits and schedule to see if they are useful now? Do we try to gain as much clarity as we can get on certain issues?

All of the above questions are designed to encourage personal responsibility. By eliminating unnecessary problems and taking as much control over our life as possible we can filter out unnecessary difficulties so our minds, hearts, and bodies can be free enough to move further in the spiritual life. To appreciate grace and our dependence on God does not mean we shouldn't do as much as we can in our lives as well. Not to do so would be quite disrespectful to the God who empowers us.

The spiritual life is the real life. The more we can be sensitive to the distractions, illusions, and delusions we have in the way we live and relate, the deeper and more meaningful our lives can be. The more truly sensitive we can be to ourselves, the more sensitive we can be to God.

In addition, self-awareness can set the stage for us to see more clearly our own sense of God in our lives or our "personal spiritual theology" (what we believe, think, and feel about God). In this way, our psychological health can aid us to be open to the movements of grace in our lives. And, it is to this topic we turn next.

What Is Our "Personal Spiritual Theology"?

If someone were to ask you to draw an image of God in your mind's eye, you might initially draw a blank or claim you are not a very imaginative person. But, imaginative or not, there is a view you have about God—a personal spiritual theology—which shapes your faith and in turn determines what kind of an active person of hope you will be when faced with a sense of darkness.

Consequently, transforming our implicit sense of God into a more explicit one is a good first step toward grasping our spiritual theology and increasing our sensitivity to God. By doing this we can also be clearer about who stands with us in our interior or exterior darkness, as well as in our times of joy and peace.

Once we have a greater appreciation of our beliefs and our relationship with God, we will be able to read scripture and pray with more meaning and vigor. Bringing our image of God into dialogue with those images of the Ultimate in the Bible will help us to open ourselves to a truer sense of who God can be in our lives.

Once we do this, our prayer can be more realistic. We are not merely praying to a figure of no consequence or position in our lives. Instead, we are encountering the Holy, and we know it. We are not playing hide-and-seek with a fleeting, vague God, but interacting with the Lord personally and concretely. We are like those people who met Jesus when his words and deeds made an impact on this earth. Just as his presence had a peaceful effect on the lonely, confused hearts of the people of his day, so too it has on ours.

To surface and sharpen the focus of God within our hearts now, there are any number of questions we can ask as part of the process of clarifying our spiritual theology. This will determine the basic attitude we have toward God and in turn help us see what we believe the Lord's feelings are toward us. The following are only offered as a helpful beginning in this pursuit. As in the other lists in this chapter, it may be helpful to reflect on them now and again periodically in the future. In addition, they may trigger other questions or areas which impact how we see God in life, our life.

Clarifying Our Personal Spiritual Theology

1) When I think of God, what are the images that flash through my mind? (Quickly jotting responses to this and the following questions may prove useful to those who wish to use their answers as a record to chart the movements in their spiritual life.)

2) Given these images, what do I expect of God when I feel depressed, stressful, confused, lost, frightened, angry, sad, or worried?

3) If I were trying to describe who God is to my closest friend, what would I say?

4) Is there any difference that my personal relationship with God makes in my life? If so, specifically what are these differences in various situations?

5) What affective interpersonal style was predominant in my family? Were people physically demonstrative in their love? In their anger? Were they at home with their own sexuality? How were my parents different in the way they related to others affectively? In my style of relating to others, who am I more like—my mother, father, or some other significant person present during my growing-up years?

Given this understanding, how do I affectively relate? Am I able to be angry, respectful, distant, intimate with God? Under what circumstances do I relate to God like the parent (or significant person present in my household during the early formative years) who I am least like emotionally?

6) What do I believe God thinks about me? How does God really feel about me?

7) Do I view myself as God sees me? If not, what's the difference and in what way does this impact my relationship with God and the world?

8) With whom in my life do I relate most closely to the way in which I relate to God? What does this say about my relationship with God?

9) How do I feel God is acting/not acting in my life? How have I experienced grace in my life? Is such a phenomenon common or unusual for me?

10) What is the word which would best describe my relationship with God? How is this different than what I would hope this relationship would be? What am I doing about this/planning to do?

11) How does my image of, and relationship with, God affect my relationship with/attitude toward:

a) difficult situations,

b) closest friends,

c) people I dislike,

d) family,

e) colleagues,

f) friends,

g) my ideals,

h) my fears,

i) my work,

j) my free time (weekends, evenings, coffee breaks, vacations ...),

12) Do I take my sense of covenant (deep relationship) with God seriously? If not, why not? If so, how is it reflected in my actions during the day? My choices? My lifestyle?

The above questions are part and parcel of developing a greater awareness of who this God is in our lives. We are putting ourselves in Peter's place when Jesus asked of him: "Who do you say that I am?" and realizing that our answers will say as much about us as they do about God.

As we come to grips with this, it becomes more important to take time out each day to make God a more intimate part of our lives. Certainly we do this through regular prayer and a periodic taking stock of our spiritual theology. But we also must deepen our awareness of God in our lives by trying to see *how* God is present and active in our lives, a process generally referred to as "theological reflection."

Seeing God as Part of Our Lives

Much has been written about the topic of theological reflection to help people understand how to better include God in their daily lives. (The Whiteheads' book *Method in Ministry*[1] is a classic and Robert Kinast's work on theological reflection[2] is another very practical, valuable, and worthy review of the process.) But for those of us who don't have the time or theological background to delve into such material more fully, there are some very simple steps worth delineating. They can enable all of us to immediately improve the few moments we spend in the evening reflecting on our day.

With a simple and clear structure which is easy to remember, I think we are more apt to make theological reflection a more natural part of our lives. This is essential to improving the quality of our day and it sets the stage for those times when bigger issues or crises enter our lives. When serious problems arise we can apply the process we have been using. We can also benefit from the insights God has already helped us gain from our having been attentive all along to the place of grace in our daily activities and interactions.

The elements of theological reflection vary somewhat. They also depend upon the tradition of the spiritual guide with whom we might consult or the authors we regularly read on this topic. However, many would agree that the process includes at least the following elements in some form:

1) Determine the most important, concrete occurrence during the day.

2) Image oneself being back in the event and recall it in as much detail as possible while reflecting on how you were feeling, thinking, and behaving at the time.

3) Establish why this particular event had such a personally-felt impact.

4) Relate it to scripture as best as you can. Think about the New Testament and ask: "What would Jesus have done in these circumstances?" Or, "What do I believe Jesus would say to me now if he were here?"

5) Establish what you feel you can learn from it on a deep spiritual level (and if possible write it down in a copybook you save to journal in the evening).

6) Put the new-found insights gained from reflection into action with a specific plan for the future.

So, a good reflection that brings God into our lives includes: recalling concrete events that had an impact (either positive or negative); the use of imagery; a simple application of scripture; and a willingness to learn from the interaction in a way that will lead to action.

Also, although it is important to be involved in this process in a setting of silence and solitude at day's end, it is essential wherever possible to share the fruits of such reflections with others in order to get the benefit of other objective thoughts and views. There is no substitute for being a person who is regularly reflective with an eye to sacred scripture; but there are also so many ways to delude ourselves. Consequently, feedback from valued friends who are willing to be both supportive and challenging to us is necessary as well.

This is why we need a faith community of family, friends, and/or colleagues with whom we feel free to reveal ourselves and wonder over the obvious and mysterious ways God meets us in our lives. In this way theological reflection can feed, enliven, and keep relevant our personal spiritual theology.

What Is God's Will in Specific Circumstances?

Living sensitively today relies then on: being psychologically responsible, having a good sense of one's personal spiritual theology, and practicing theological reflection in a natural, ongoing way each day. In this way we can welcome God as a true part of our lives in a manner that encourages us to stay honest, clear-headed, involved, at peace, and compassionate.

Another helpful way to be sensitive to God is through regularly seeking God's will for us in specific circumstances (discernment). Accordingly, it is essential for us to address the topic of "spiritual discernment" if we wish to be able to have enough sensitivity, clarity, and strength to do what is right, especially when so much seems to be going wrong in so many people's lives.

Discernment is clearly a spiritual exercise and is commonly defined as "the process, associated with the virtue of prudence, by which we try to decide what God wills us to do in these particular circumstances and for the future."[3] Discernment is a process in which we seek to be open to seeing whether the call to action we hear each day and in life in general is from God, or whether some other voices (tradition, society, family ...) are guiding it. While the process of theological reflection (which we just noted) seeks to help us learn from the past, discernment is primarily concerned with responding to God now and in the future.

Discernment is first and foremost a gift from God—one which should not be taken for granted through passivity on our part. Even when we unequivocally affirm the paramount place of God and the movement of grace in our lives, this does not relieve us from giving careful attention to the human dimension of "radical openness" to the messages of God. The well-known Ignatian tenet "work as if everything depended on you, but pray as if everything depended upon God" is at the very basis of discernment. The "work" in discernment is to do everything in our power to be open to the Truth, to God, and to attempt to appreciate our inherent resistance to change so we can let go and allow the Spirit of God to lead.

John Haughey, in his classic book on the Holy Spirit, emphasizes this point:

> A life of complete faith propels one to live not by his own ideas, impulses, or abilities, but by the leadings of the Spirit that have much the same ebb and flow and unpredictability that the wind and waves do. ... It is scary to say "Yes" to being possessed. It is easier to possess. It is beautiful to receive the Presence of the Other but difficult to let Him remain Other.[4]

Discernment is neither a simple nor direct process. To think so is to be naive or religiously imprudent. There are many issues that make discernment an elusive and humbling experience.

First, the Spirit itself is invisible and transcendent. Secondly, we are prone to rationalize in our own favor—i.e., to highlight those elements which support our predispositions toward one or another course of action and to ignore those elements which work against that disposition. Thirdly, many issues are complicated and do not admit to ready solutions.[5]

And so, when discerning for oneself or in guiding someone else there are a number of elements which need to be appreciated if this spiritual decision-making process is to be true to its purpose. Moreover, particularly with respect to the second factor listed above (our tendency to be more defensive than usual—e.g., to rationalize—in certain circumstances), this may involve the use of the insights of the social and behavioral sciences.

This is not to say that discernment is in any way subordinate to the psychological or sociological enterprise, but as the noted theologian Karl Rahner aptly pointed out in his essay "Theology and Anthropology," anything that can bring clarity to the human situation is relevant to a theological undertaking. With respect to discernment in particular, Ernest Larkin puts it even more directly and reflects Ignatius of Loyola's emphasis on the need to employ every technique possible to gather appropriate information for reflection: "Discernment is ... open to new developments in theological understanding such as the insights of depth psychology and social analysis."[6]

Making a decision in faith, then, can be assisted by the behavioral and social sciences. Insights from these disciplines can help us be sensitive to what is promoting diffidence or perhaps blocking us from seeking the Truth, interpreting events in light of the gospel, and acting in faith upon what we have just learned.

Clarity

With respect to sensitivity to God, clarity is especially relevant as a way of opening ourselves to the Truth:

> Clarity helps us to face almost any issue or person and feel the force of the biblical injunction, "Be not afraid." It is the source of a healthy attitude toward life. With clarity, our actions become psychologically sound and spiritually responsive.

Yet most of us consciously and unconsciously avoid seeing the Light. This may sound ridiculous, since being clear is so akin to being fully aware, fully alive. However, the process involved in seeing life clearly requires a good deal of focused energy and often forces us to give up many of our nostalgic illusions.

Clarity is not something that can be limited. The same perceptive light that pierces the shroud that is preventing better understanding of others and God simultaneously shines through the darkness of the denials we make about our own nature, our own style of living. In seeing everything clearly then, we must, by definition of this encountering process, see our own games as well. This is not something we are used to doing. We often hide things from ourselves, and unconsciously we certainly often try to deceive others. ...

Still, the effort to honestly face ourselves is essential. If we don't avoid or give up, if we don't panic when faced with the reality of our personal games, much personal restoration and power are possible. The point is that once we understand, we can accept; once we accept, we can be open to being healed and open to the role we all have in healing others. What more can we ask of a process if it can produce such results? What better journey can we take if this be the ongoing reward of such a quest. ...

Being clear, then, is the act of gaining a Christian perspective on our life. This is a life in relationship: relationship with self, others, and God. Such a perspective will cause both tension and peace; such a perspective is also contextual—it is very much cradled in the past, present, and our view of the future. Finally, it requires the stamina, discipline, patience, humility, and courage to be a critical thinker in light of the Gospel and the exemplary ministry of Christ.[7]

Not wanting to be clear about some thing or issue which would cause us discomfort or pain is nothing new. There is always a natural, unconscious desire to avoid, deny, repress, or distort material that might cause internal conflict. Insight can and often does hurt. This is beautifully illustrated in the reflection of Jack Nelson, who, while walking the streets of Calcutta, thought to himself, "The poverty so enraged me that I wanted to scream at God. Then I came to a painful realization. In the suffering of the poor, God was screaming at me."[8]

So, while steps to thinking clearly at some level might not be quite palatable, they are important to provide us with a framework for channeling the healthy motivation people have in the service of uncovering the truth. Therefore, assistance in this area should be welcomed by those seeking to do all they can when discerning the will of God for themselves (and would also be a worthwhile area for study by spiritual directors and counselors.)

In his classic 1933 book *How We Think* John Dewey presented a basic problem-solving outline designed to help people who wish to be clearer in their decision-making activities. In it he emphasized the following simple steps:

- Recognize you have a problem,
- Then analyze it,
- Open up possible solutions,
- Test the consequences,
- Judge the solution selected.[9]

Since his early work, a number of other "critical thinkers" who have sought better ways to problem-solve have joined Dewey in his efforts. We in our efforts at spiritual discernment must have the courage as well to question— really question—our positions and beliefs so we can seek to be clear in our prayerful, sensitive search for God's will. As I have noted elsewhere:

With ... courageous trust we try to emulate critical thinkers by seeking to ask ourselves the following types of questions:

- Am I seeking to see things in black and white, or am I willing to appreciate the ambiguity—the "grays"—of things?

- Do I just seek answers, even in those areas where there are none to be had?

- Do I try to see how my views of self, others, and God correspond to the reality of others? In other words, do I critique my attitudes and beliefs so that I don't slip into secure delusions?

- Am I slow to believe and not subject merely to rhetoric or convenient conclusions? Am I able to hold onto the possible as well as the probable without pain?

- Am I able to enter into the mystery of the unfolding of Jesus being revealed to me, or am I looking for cookbook approaches to life?

- Do I gravitate toward the quick solution or one side of an issue because I lack the intellectual stamina and solid theology of hope that encourages an open mind and an open heart?

- Am I so afraid of failure and rejection by others that I go along with what opinion I perceive as current rather than the one I perceive as more in line with the Gospel? ...

- Am I truly open to a repeated conversion of my beliefs, my attitudes—my heart—or do I resist the disturbing chill of the fresh air that must come in when I open my heart and mind's door to the Spirit? More specifically, am I willing to examine unpleasant personal thoughts, impulses, and feelings so that I can find out more about myself and the direction I am moving in life?[10]

Trying to be clear can be dangerous to the status quo, to our normal ways of thinking and viewing the world. It interrupts our automatic acceptance of so-called "common sense" and makes us ask "Why?" or "Why not?" when others just go along almost without thinking about life, their life. When our thinking process is on "automatic pilot" we certainly cannot live a sensitive, reflective life—the life of the gospel.

We can sometimes see this when a writer alters a saying which has drifted through the ages untested. This wakes us up to the fact that traditionalism, rather than a respect for tradition, is keeping some portion of the population back. Too often racism, ageism, sexism, and other types of prejudice designed to deflate others' self-esteem is based on accepted aphorisms which need to be examined, turned upside down, and laughed about. Only then can we see that they contain the seeds of destruction, not wisdom. Maybe that is what was partially behind Gloria Steinem's Zen-like quip (which I must confess I love): "A woman without a man is like a fish without a bicycle."

With respect to our spirituality clarity in our thinking process can cut to the core of idolatry and bring new light to discernment. Too often discernment is confined by a misguided, uncritical loyalty to the tradition and religious imagery we have been given.

To give a sense of this (and to close this section of the chapter), I offer the following two dialogues from Anthony de Mello's book *One Minute Wisdom*:

> Belief
>
> The Master had quoted Aristotle: "In the quest of truth it would seem better and indeed necessary to give up what is dearest to us." And he substituted the word "God" for "truth."
>
> Later a disciple said to him, "I am ready, in the quest for God, to give up anything: wealth, friends, family, country, life itself. What else can a person give up?

The Master calmly replied, "One's beliefs about God."

The disciple went away sad, for he clung to his convictions. He feared "ignorance" more than death.[11]

Idolatry

The Master never wearied of warning his disciples about the dangers of religion. He loved to tell the story of the prophet who carried a flaming torch through the streets, saying he was going to set fire the temple so that people would concern themselves more with the Lord than with the temple.

Then he would add, "Someday I shall carry a flaming torch myself to set fire to both the temple and the Lord."[12]

How Psychology Can Also Be of Help in Discerning God's Will

In addition to the preceding reflections on clarity and decision making, I would like to offer some further reflections from psychology. From the vantage point of clinical psychology and psychiatry, I believe that these insights would be helpful to persons interested in spiritual growth. They are drawn from cognitive therapy literature, a school of thought which is very interested in helping people to be as accurate as possible in how they view the world.

Perception is very powerful. How we view ourselves and the world will determine to a great extent how we feel and behave. Anthony de Mello, in one of my favorite dialogues from his books, points this out when he says,

To a disciple who was forever complaining about others the Master said, "If it is peace you want, seek to change yourself, not other people. It is easier to protect your feet with slippers than to carpet the whole earth."[13]

Given the importance of a person's outlook, I have no doubt that the insights of the cognitive therapy school would have value for any of us. Certainly spiritual directors, when dealing with persons in discernment at certain crisis stages of their lives who express that everything seems dark, can benefit from them.

The cognitive principles laid out by Aaron Beck[14] and his associates, and further popularized by David Burns in his book *Feeling Good*, are of particular relevance. These investigators and clinicians have focused particularly on how distorted thinking and illogical beliefs can lead to depressive or negative emotions. Being aware of some of their tenets and applying them at an elementary level can help us to discern the difference between illogical, self-defeating thinking (a psychological issue), and a period of spiritual impasse when we are truly experiencing spiritual desolation or the "dark night."[15]

For spiritual directors and those who wish to be better spiritual friends to each other, a little bit of knowledge about the principles of cognitive therapy can be a powerful thing. For instance, knowing how systematic negative perceptions can maintain depression or anxiety can lead us in our prayer life. It can also help directors to question thinking styles and test the accuracy of the predictions and interpretations based on such thinking and beliefs. In a case of mild depressive thinking, this may cut through the psychological difficulty sufficiently enough to surface the spiritual issues which need to be faced. In other cases, it may uncover the extent of a psychological problem to the point where some counseling may be a good idea.

To provide a sense of what I am referring to, the following several common distortions from Burn's book *Feeling Good* illustrate how people (and I would add especially perfectionistic Christians) fall prey to thinking errors that cause depressive feelings and an overall sense of discouragement:

- *All-or-nothing thinking*: You see things in black-and-white categories. If your performance falls short of perfect, you see yourself as a total failure. ...
- *Overgeneralization:* You see a single negative event as a never-ending pattern of defeat. ...

- *Disqualifying the positive:* You reject positive experiences by insisting that they "don't count" for some reason or other. In this way you can maintain a negative belief that is contradicted by your everyday experience. ...

- *Emotional reasoning:* You assume that your negative emotions necessarily reflect the way things are: "I feel it, therefore it must be true. ..."

- *Should statements:* You try to motivate yourself with shoulds and shouldn'ts. ... The emotional consequence is guilt. When you direct should statements toward others, you feel anger, frustration, and resentment. ...

- *Personalization:* You see yourself as the cause of some negative external event which in fact you were not primarily responsible for.[16]

At the very least, then, cognitive psychotherapeutic principles such as the ones above can aid us (and the persons we walk with in life) to think as clearly as possible and be alert for erroneous beliefs and distorted thinking patterns. These may be general in nature or tied to certain incorrect beliefs. Facing them aggressively is essential so unnecessary darkness doesn't distort our self-image. Such beliefs and ways of thinking can hold back a vibrant, challenging discernment and result in our burying our talents rather than investing them in life—our life and the lives of others.

Once again, it would be good for us to remember that one of the greatest gifts we can share with others in pain, despair, or confusion is a clear sense of our own peace and knowledge that we are loved. In discernment and in darkness we must always see how our thinking may be affecting our moods. If we are depressed emotionally, or feel useless or inadequate, it may not be a spiritual movement at all. It may well be a psychological one which we can and should directly address.

During the day, we often move too quickly from A (the event) to C (the feeling) and forget to examine B (our distorted associations). For instance, we may fail at something, a friend may be angry with us, or we may lose a cherished goal. These are the events. Later we may feel terrible—either "down" or somewhat "gray." We may think it is the failure, interpersonal misunderstanding, or loss that is causing us to feel so depressed or confused. But it really isn't. It is our unexamined associations that are feeding a hidden, exaggerated, negative belief about ourselves.

In the case of the failure at something, for instance, we may be saying to ourselves, "If I failed at this, then I am a failure." We may not even think to question this falsely-based self-talk. Without knowing it we are transforming a possible embarrassment, source of awkwardness, or feeling of guilt about a real event into a source of unnecessary shame about ourselves as persons. This is a psychological cancer attacking our self-image which we must fight vigorously so our spirit can remain vibrant in a lost world so desperately depending on us to remind it that God loves us.

As a result, we need to be aware of our negative feelings, trace them back to the events, and look at our own often ridiculous and exaggerated associations. Then we can add a D (a disputation of them) to our understanding of the A (event), B (associations), and C (feelings) sequence of our thinking process. While doing this may not make us feel better immediately, we will have a framework to confront our unnecessary darkness. The new correct thinking will also seed more accurate beliefs about ourselves. This is good; in a very basic sense, it is also holy.

In the end, the wheat of sound spiritual self-esteem will grow abundantly. The chaff of unnecessary self-condemnation and the temptation to withdraw from the call to be a sensitive person in these times will wither. The chaff, to be sure, will always be present. But it won't be strong enough to choke off the truth of Jesus' claim to us in John 15:14, "You are my friends."

The Final Word in Facing the Darkness: Grace

I have emphasized our real responsibility to be as clear as possible when we face spiritual decisions in life. In the service of such clarity various ideas and approaches have been offered as possible aids in our efforts to cooperate with grace and embrace our dependence on God. Yet at the same time we must work as if everything depended on us.

In today's complex and duplicitous world, where the gospel of Christ can become so easily rationalized and domesticated, all efforts must be made to be open and clear, to face the Truth. Any help that psychology can offer us should and must be welcomed. There is an important place for knowledge about how skills in increasing our self-awareness, developing a clearer personal spiritual theology, knowing and applying a practical beginning approach to theological reflection, and seeing the roles critical thinking and cognitive therapeutic literature play in discernment.

Grace is to be recognized and greeted with all of the energy, knowledge, and willingness we can muster. Otherwise it will be so missed, taken for granted, or willfully ignored due to our narcissism or anxiety. Burying our talents in these difficult, needy times is a subtle form of sinfulness that no one can afford. To do so is not only foolish, but also dangerous—for ourselves and the needy world in which we live.

However, discernment, true self-awareness, appreciating our personal theology, and theological reflection are *spiritual* movements—this point can't be emphasized enough. Without grace, without God, there is no true process of sensitively discerning who we are and who we are called to be.

But it is also true that there are times when all of the careful problem-solving in the world will achieve nothing. We are at an impasse. This is a time of special appreciation of our dependence on God's mercy and guidance. It is a time for prayer, true prayer. It is also a time for patience, trust in the Lord, and a sense of alertness to the new ways God may be calling us to find *the* Way in a darkness we can't control, remove, or analyze. The simple spiritual reality is that God will provide the light, in the way and at the time, that God's providence, not a human time frame, determines. We are free, but we often forget that God is too.

If we wait and don't run, we will see what we need to see. If we stay and don't try to distract or numb ourselves, we will hear what we must hear. And if we hold onto our hope and don't drown ourselves under rumination over the ruined expectations, if we open ourselves when our grieving for what we have lost is done, then we will experience what we really need. We will be given what we can receive now, so we may become deeper persons on our journey.

If we remain sensitive to the presence of God in faith and in prayer, and in the darkness of confusion and suffering, the darkness will teach us, it will become the light. And with a new, graced sense of simplicity we will have the ability to be sensitive to this different light and recognize it for what it truly is: the love of God present to us at a time when we most need a spiritual companion to help us on our road to Emmaus. It is a road with necessary crosses but, just as certainly, a road to real resurrection.

Epilogue:
A Person Without Guile

There is a great deal of darkness in the world. We don't need anyone to tell us this sad reality. A great deal of this is horrible and we must do all we can to face and correct it. In some ways, the darkness is like a forest fire—needed to clear the way for new growth but no less devastating for those of us who must endure it.

We need to name the darkness and understand what it is telling us. Then, once we have the diagnosis, we must act and act boldly. But how can we do this if we are trapped in the darkness, mired in despair, confusion, and anxiety within our own hearts? What if we refuse the honesty that is the fuel of an energetic, simple life of a sensitive person of faith?

Virginia Woolf once remarked: "If you do not tell the truth about yourself, you cannot tell it about other people."[1] Maybe this is why we seek simple, honest, sensitive people (persons without guile) for advice, guidance, and words of true wisdom. But, upon reflection, we have to ask: Is it really their words that cut through the pollution of our lies and the games we play with ourselves, others, and God? Or, is it their modeling of what it is like to be whole, integrated, and simple in their prayer, self-appreciation, and interactions with others—their total sensitivity to God, self, and others— that most inspires and challenges us?

In scripture we read how people naturally prefer the darkness to the light. In psychology we see how persons ask for honest feedback and seek a cure through therapy, but their actions often show an unconscious wish for relief, escape, and no real change. This is not unusual. As a matter of fact, don't we often fall into this trap ourselves? Aren't we sometimes fearful of being revealed for who we really feel we are?

Still, both these inner fears and the darkness in the world—social, psychological, religious, environmental, physical, and spiritual—are not reasons to give up. Paradoxically, they are an impetus to be even more sensitive by looking harder for God in interpersonal situations, others, ourselves, and during our prayerful times of silence and solitude.

Of course we will be discouraged at times, of course we will experience the pain of injustice. Not to do so would be tantamount to being spiritually dead. Women in particular must face this pain of injustice. One theologian, reflecting on sexism, went as far as to note:

It is logical that all women within patriarchy should experience depression, and in varying degrees. Indeed, given the prevailing conditions, it is almost cause for alarm if a woman never feels depressed.[2]

And so, we all must face the trap of despair and the temptation for withdrawal. We must embrace the necessary cross of honest sensitivity to ourselves and God so we can better know what is true and continue to bring God's light into the world by being sensitive to others in need.

For years we have heard: "Children close their ears to advice, but open their eyes to example." What will our example be? If we feel our example must be total perfection and success, we will only run away. The odds are too great and we are too frail. Like the suffering professionals in ministry, medicine, and mental health I cited in the beginning of the book, all of us need to remember that if we expect perfection of ourselves, then our sensitivity will be too limited. Our compassion will become compulsive, or confined only to little tentative steps into the darkness of others' lives.

We are "simply" called to be faithful, open, hopeful, self-aware, present ... to be sensitive persons without guile. But being without guile isn't the same as being without sin. Instead, it is an attitude of simplicity which leads us to become keenly aware of who we are, to acknowledge and embrace our identity so it is possible to greet grace with humility and to stand with others in their darkness without illusion.

During her late adolescent years my daughter Michaele once said to me in a burst of candor: "When I was very young, everything had to be so 'nice' at the dinner table, and I didn't want to come. Now, I feel when we come together we can be real and say what we feel. We can even disagree! One or both of us may get angry but I know that it is all right. Now I want to come to dinner to be with you and Mom, and this makes me happy."

The honest words of an adolescent, sensitive to herself and her parents, cut to the heart of the matter. They show us at a deeper level what we already know: that hypocrisy, "good" family images, and the deception marked by "chronic niceness" prevent the possibility for real intimacy and growth in many instances. They remind us that darkness outside of ourselves is only dangerous when we are steeped in secrets (even from ourselves as in the case of subtle characterological sin) and continue to hide what we believe to be the darkness within ourselves, our family, our church, and our country.

In my daughter's words (which said we could be free of playing games and putting on psychological disguises) I could hear echoes of God's words in the garden when Adam and Eve were ashamed. God asked: "Who told you that you were naked?" Or, in today's language: "Who told you that you needed to make believe you are something other than you are? I know you as you really are and love you; why do you not believe me?"

This book has been less about confronting the troubles out in the world than it has been about the call of God to be sensitive persons who can embrace the joys of life as well as face the darkness that remains within us.

Being a sensitive presence in the world depends on this. It relies on our being attuned to the real problems we encounter in life with an embrace of real hope (like the displaced Vietnamese people I encountered along the Mekong river in Cambodia did.) The source of such hope is God's promise to me, to us. It is reflected in the lives of holy, simple, sensitive people who are quietly purifying the world of lies, greed, competition, and abuse. And, though we are far from perfect and have many faults (which we should own and seek to correct), that hope is also reflected in the goodness in us—if only we have the courage to sensitively look within, and the gratitude for all we have been blessed with by God.

And so, our sins and gifts must be honestly embraced together. We must be willing to be naked again before our God, in humility and trust. We must believe we are loved for who we are and desire deeply to see who we can be with a bit more clarity and the courage to live each day in God's good grace.

The sensitive light in the darkness that I have written about here is anchored in the words of Jesus which are so beautifully brought together in the following refrain from David Haas' song "You Are Mine." And, it is with these words from the Lord that I close. In sharing them I hope we can both remember and take them to heart, so that no matter how terrible we might feel for the moment, or how bleak the world might be at any point, we will know that the darkness will never prevail. Never.

> Do not be afraid.
> I am with you.
> I have called you each by name.
> Come follow me, I will bring you home.
> I love you … you are mine.[3]

Endnotes

Introduction

1. Edwina Gately, "Healing, Nurturing, Birthing," *SEDOS Research Seminar*, Vol. 23, Nos. 6 and 7, May 1991, Rome: 15th June and 15th July, p. 206.

2. Gately, pp. 206, 207.

3. Abraham Heschel, *Who Is Man?*, Stanford, CA: Stanford University Press, p. 96.

Chapter One

1. Maya Angelou shared this story during a three-day symposium, "Understanding Evil," held at the Institute for the Humanities, Saldo, Texas.

2. Erik Erikson, *Children and Society* (Second Edition), New York: Norton, 1963, p. 269.

3. Robert Wicks, *Availability: The Problem and the Gift*, Mahwah, NJ: Paulist, 1986, p. 5.

4. A slightly different version of this story appears in Anthony de Mello, *Awareness*, New York: Doubleday, 1990, p. 28.

5. This and any other case material presented in this book are composites and/or fictionalized rather than actual accounts.

6. Quoted in *The Last Word*, Carolyn Warner, ed., Englewood Cliffs, NJ: Prentice Hall, 1992, p. 29.

7. I am grateful to Br. Kevin Strong, F.S.C. for sharing this story with me. Additional Hassidic tales can be found in Martin Buber's *Tales of the Hassidim Early Masters*, New York: Shochen Books, 1947.

8. Robert Johnson, *Owning Your Shadow*, San Francisco: Harper Collins, 1992, pp. 64, 65.

9. Madonna Kohlbenschlag, *Lost in the Land of Oz*, San Francisco: Harper & Row, 1988, p. 41.

10. For a broader treatment of Dorothee Soelle's views on suffering, see her books: *Suffering* (Philadelphia: Fortress, 1973); *The Strength of the Weak*

(Philadelphia: Westminster Press, 1984); and *The Wisdom of Vulnerability* (Minneapolis: Fortress Press, 1990).

11. Vaclav Havel, "Idealism," *Esquire* Vol. 120, No. 4 (October, 1993), p. 68. I am grateful to Joyce Rupp for bringing this quote to my attention.

Chapter Two

1. Source unknown.

2. Anthony de Mello, *The Way to Love*, New York: Doubleday, 1992, p. 66.

3. Kahlil Gibran, *Sand and Foam*, New York: Alfred A. Knopf, 1926, p. 78.

4. Dag Hammerskjold, *Markings*, New York: Knopf, 1964, p. 55.

5. Thomas Merton, *My Argument with the Gestapo*, New York: Doubleday, 1941, pp. 160-161.

6. I am grateful to Michael Crichton whose entertaining novel, *Jurassic Park* (New York: Ballantine Books, 1990, pp. 170-171) presents such a simple explanation of "fractal."

7. Charlotte Gilman wrote this in her introductory notes to the journal, *The Forerunner*, Vol. 2, No. 9, September 1911, p. 2.

8. Nikos Kazantzakis, *Zorba the Greek*, New York: Ballantine Books, 1952, p. 300.

9. Stephen Covey, *The Seven Habits of Highly Effective People*, New York: Simon and Schuster, 1989, pp. 30-31.

Chapter Three

1. Ann Clark, "Alternate Meditation" in Anne Wilson Schaef, *Meditations for Women Who Do Too Much*, San Francisco: Harper Collins, 1990, no pagination.

2. Ruth Benedict, *Patterns of Culture*, Boston: Houghton-Mifflin, 1934, pp. 10, 11.

3. Audre Lorde, quoted on March 4th in *Meditations for Women Who Do Too Much*.

4. Dietrich Bonhoeffer, *Letters and Papers from Prison*, edited by Eberhard Bethge, New York: Macmillan, 1972, p. 376.

5. Benjamin Hoff, *The Te of Piglet*, New York: Dutton, 1992, pp. 67-69.

6. I am grateful to Ferdinand Lansang, O.Carm., for sharing this story with me.

7. Sallie McFague, *Models of God*, Philadelphia: Fortress Press, 1987, see chapter 6: "God as Friend." I am grateful to Ed Bailey for bringing this to my attention.

8. I am grateful to Professor David Augsburger of Fuller Theological Seminary for sharing with me this abbreviated paraphrase from a presentation given by him at the Los Angeles Religious Education Congress. For those who wish to read "The Tale of the Barber's Sixth Brother" in its entirety, an excellent critical translation can be found in *Tales from the Thousand and One Nights*, translated with an introduction by N.J. Dawood, Middlesex, England: Penguin Books, 1973, pp. 68-76.

9. Thomas Merton, *Conjectures of a Guilty Bystander*, New York: Doubleday, 1965, p. 145.

10. I am thankful to Jeff Dauses for this funny little insight.

Chapter Four

1. I am grateful to my wife Michaele for her help in breaking open the Word in doing an exegesis of this passage from Luke.

2. Janet Ruffing, "Seeing in the Dark," *Review for Religious*, vol. 51, no. 2 (April, May), pp. 236-248. Dr. Ruffing does a wonderful job of speaking about darkness in this article. With respect to this section, she also relies on the work of Joann Conn in her book *Spirituality and Personal Maturity*, Mahwah, New Jersey: Paulist, 1989, and on Constance Fitzgerald's fine article "Impasse and the Dark Night of the Soul" in *Living with the Apocalypse*, edited by Tilden Edwards, New York: Harper and Row, 1984.

3. Jeffrey Kottler, *On Being a Therapist*, San Francisco: Jossey-Bass, 1986, p. 8.

Chapter Five

1. George Sand reputedly noted this in an issue of *A Critic at Large* which has long been out of print.

2. James Finley, *Merton's Palace of Nowhere*, Notre Dame: Ave Maria Press, 1978, p. 117.

3. Thomas Merton, quoted in Michael Mott's, *The Seven Mountains of Thomas Merton*, Boston: Houghton-Mifflin, 1984, p. 263.

4. Henri Nouwen, *Genesee Diary*, New York: Doubleday, 1976, p. 71.

5. Thomas Aldrich, "Leaves from a Notebook," *The Works of Thomas Bailey Aldrich*, Boston: The Jefferson Press, 1903, p. 14.

6. Jean Anouilh, *The Rehearsal*, New York: Coward-McCann, 1961, p. 72.

7. Lionel Blue, *Lionel Blue*, Springfield, IL: Templegate, 1987, p. 28.

8. Kahlil Gibran, *Sand and Foam*, p. 45.

9. Jean-Jacques Rousseau, *The Confessions of Jean-Jacques Rousseau*, New York: The Heritage Press, 1955, p. 15.

10. William Blake, "The Marriage of Heaven and Hell," *The Complete Poetry and Prose of William Blake*, revised edition, edited by David V. Erdman, Los Angeles: University of California Press, p. 35.

11. Henri Nouwen's book, *The Way of the Heart*, New York: Seabury, 1977, gives a full treatment of this topic.

12. Kenneth Leech, *Experiencing God*, San Francisco: Harper & Row, 1985, p. 140.

13. Thomas Merton, *The Wisdom of the Desert*, New York: New Directions, 1960, p. 20.

14. Paul Tillich, source unknown.

15. Anthony Bloom, *Beginning to Pray*, Ramsey, NJ: Paulist, 1970.

16. Thomas Merton, *A Vow of Conversation*, edited by Naomi Burton, New York: Farrar, Straus, Giroux, 1988, p. 152.

17. Gertrude Mueller Nelson, *Here All Dwell Free: Stories to Heal the Wounded Feminine*, New York: Doubleday, 1991, p. 62.

18. Karl Menninger, source unknown.

19. This story by Anthony de Mello, and many other good ones, are contained in Tabor Publishing's videotape, *Wake Up! Spirituality for Today*.

20. John Eudes Bamberger, cited in Henri Nouwen, *Genesee Diary*, p. 119.

21. Anonymous.

Chapter Six

1. Evelyn Eaton Whitehead and James D. Whitehead, *Method in Ministry*, San Francisco: Harper San Francisco, 1985.

2. Robert L. Kinast, *Let the Ministry Teach: A Handbook for Theological Reflection*, FL: Center for Theological Reflection.

3. Richard P. McBrien., *Catholicism*, Minneapolis: Winston, 1980, p. xxvii.

4. John C. Haughey, *The Conspiracy of God: The Holy Spirit in Men*, New York: Doubleday, 1973, pp. 62, 112.

5. McBrien, p. 980.

6. Ernest E. Larkin, "Discernment of Spirits," *The Westminster Dictionary of Christian Spirituality*, Gordon S. Wakefield, ed., Philadelphia: Westminster, 1983, p. 116.

7. Robert J. Wicks, *Availability*, pp. 25-27.

8. Jack Nelson, *Hunger for Justice*, Maryknoll, NY: Orbis, 1990, p. vii.

9. John Dewey, *How We Think*, New York: D. C. Heath, 1933.

10. Wicks, pp. 36-37.

11. Anthony de Mello, *One Minute Wisdom*, New York: Doubleday, 1985, p. 119.

12. de Mello, p. 143.

13. de Mello, p. 38.

14. Aaron T. Beck, A. John Rush, Brian F. Shaw, and Gary Emery, *Cognitive Therapy of Depression*, New York: Guilford Press, 1979.

15. Constance Fitzgerald, "Impasse and the Dark Night," *Living with the Apocalypse*, Tilden Edwards, ed., New York: Harper and Row, 1984.

16. David Burns, *Feeling Good: The New Mood Therapy*, New York: Morrow, 1980, pp. 40-41.

Epilogue

1. Quoted in Carolyn Warner, *The Last Word*, Englewood Cliffs, NJ: Prentice-Hall, 1992, p. 56.

2. Mary Daly, *Pure Lust: Elemental Feminist Philosophy*, San Francisco: Harper and Row, 1984, p. 256.

3. David Haas, "You Are Mine," Copyright (c) 1991 by G.I.A. Publications, Inc., Chicago, Illinois. All rights reserved. Used with permission.

ABOUT THE AUTHOR

Dr. Robert Wicks is Professor and Director of Program Development for the Graduate Programs in Pastoral Counseling at Loyola College in Maryland. Dr. Wicks, who received his doctorate in psychology from Hahneman Medical College, has also taught in universities and professional schools of psychology, medicine, social work, theology, and nursing.

His major areas of expertise are the integration of psychology and spirituality, pastoral counseling, and the treatment of secondary stress disorders. His clinical practice focuses on working with psychotherapists, physicians and nurses, and persons in full-time ministry. In addition, he is a frequent lecturer in the United States, Canada, Europe, Central America, and Asia. Recently, he lectured in Thailand, Japan, Taiwan, and also worked inside Cambodia just prior to their elections. During this visit his work was with NGOs (Non-Governmental Officers) from the English-speaking international community who were present to help the Khmer people rebuild their nation following years of terror and torture.

In addition to his faculty position and clinical work, Dr. Wicks is also general editor of the *Integration Books* series (Paulist Press), a book review editor, and a member of the editorial board of *Human Development*. Dr. Wicks has written over thirty books. He is the senior co-editor of the two-volume *Clinical Handbook of Pastoral Counseling* (Paulist Press) and *Pastoral Counseling in a Global Church* (Orbis Press). His authored works include: *Touching the Holy: Ordinariness, Self-Esteem and Friendship* (Ave Maria Press); and *Seeking Perspective; Living Simply in an Anxious World;* and *Availability: The Problem and the Gift* (both from Paulist Press).

Also by Robert Wicks:

Touching the Holy
Ave Maria Press, 1992

Seeking Perspective
Paulist Press, 1991

Living Simply in an Anxious World
Paulist Press, 1988

Caring for Self...Caring for Others
Catholic Health Association, 1987

Availability
Paulist Press, 1986

Christian Introspection
Crossroad Publishing, 1983

**NEW YORK MILLS
PUBLIC LIBRARY**
401 Main Street
New York Mills, N.Y. 13417
(315)736-5391

MEMBER
MID-YORK LIBRARY SYSTEM
Utica, N.Y. 13502

120100